WAIT!
DON'T SIGN THAT CONTRACT

WAIT! DON'T SIGN THAT CONTRACT

A Financial Gameplan for the Transition into and out of Athletics for the Collegiate and Professional Athlete

Jonathan Miller, CPA

Jones Media Publishing
10645 N. Tatum Blvd. Ste. 200-166
Phoenix, AZ 85028
www.JonesMediaPublishing.com

Disclaimer:

The author strives to be as accurate and complete as possible in the creation of this book, notwithstanding the fact that the author does not warrant or represent at any time that the contents within are accurate due to the rapidly changing nature of the Internet.

While all attempts have been made to verify information provided in this publication, the Author and Publisher assume no responsibility and are not liable for errors, omissions, or contrary interpretation of the subject matter herein. The Author and Publisher hereby disclaim any liability, loss or damage incurred as a result of the application and utilization, whether directly or indirectly, of any information, suggestion, advice, or procedure in this book. Any perceived slights of specific persons, peoples, or organizations are unintentional.

In practical advice books, like anything else in life, there are no guarantees of income made. Readers are cautioned to rely on their own judgment about their individual circumstances to act accordingly. Readers are responsible for their own actions, choices, and results. This book is not intended for use as a source of legal, business, accounting or financial advice. All readers are advised to seek services of competent professionals in legal, business, accounting, and finance field.

Printed in the United States of America

ISBN-13: 978-1-945849-76-3 paperback
JMP2019.11

DEDICATION

I would like to thank my wife Penny for letting me run around chasing athletes for all these years, my children Jason and Maddie for being excited about what I do. I'd like to thank Brandon Lloyd who's friendship and loyalty as a client means the world to me and for allowing me to be part of his NFL career as well as his post-career life. Thank you to John Bronson for his insight and friendship and allowing me to help him with his post career as well and to John Skelton for his input and support of the Sports Financial Advisors Association. To Nick Lowery for his support and understanding of the athlete financial struggle and all the good he does in our community and with former players. He is an asset to our community. Matt Fish who's always given me his time and efforts, and allowed me to be part of his NBA world. To Sarah, Lise and Kristen for being the best assistants in the world and helping me take care of all my clients. Thank you to my mom for always loving the Dodgers and my dad for taking me to the Dodgers games even though he read the paper and fell asleep. Thank you to Susan Sember for her unrelenting efforts in producing, directing and everything she does in seeing a simple idea into a project I could not have even imagined and being the driving force behind the evolution of the film “Beyond the Game.” For her love of sports and her love of family and understanding how the two are hand in hand.

CONTENTS

INTRODUCTION

WAIT! DON'T SIGN THAT CONTRACT

I wish I had the opportunity to say that to every single athlete before they signed "that" contract. But this book is more than just for the athlete going pro about to sign a multi-million dollar contract; this book is for every student athlete. While you might not sign that big money deal, you will still be in a position to sign a contract. It may be for a car lease or purchase, a home purchase, an apartment rental, or an employment contract. Throughout the pages of this book I intend to provide you with guidance and direction for some of your future financial decisions.

Many times I've met with doctors, lawyers, dentists, veterinarians, and other professionals with 16 or more years of education, graduate school, degrees and certifications. However, the common question that I am asked is "why didn't they teach me this in (Medical, Law, Vet, etc) school?"

This book will give you the basics and perhaps a road map to your success. It would be impossible to create a book that addresses every possible situation, every possible outcome for your life after sports.

As a CPA I cannot possibly know every single law in the tens of thousands of pages of the IRS code. The important thing is that I know where to go to find the answer. As you cannot be expected to know everything at the age of 22, the important thing to remember is to know WHERE TO GO for the answer. More importantly, WHOM to go to for the answers you need.

During this book I will refer to the "field," which may mean for you the court, the ice, the pool, the course etc.

In his 2013 Esquire magazine interview, Kareem Abdul-Jabbar was asked about the "20 Things I wish I'd known when I was 30." He replies that he was "living his dream" and had accomplished most of what he had set out to achieve professionally, he notes that he made mistakes, "plenty of them". Here are two of the many items of advice he said he would give his 30-year-old self.

1 BE MORE OUTGOING. He states that he would tell the "nerdy" Kareem to suck it up… and "in the immortal words of Capt. Jean-Luc Piccard, "engage!". I will discuss this later in a chapter on NETWORKING.

#3 BECOME FINANCIALLY LITERATE. He states that "dude, where's my money," is a rallying cry for many ex-athletes. There are those that suffer from unwise investments or crazy spending, he was the one that was part of the "didn't pay attention group." He chose his financial advisor because other athletes were using that same person, who, it turns out, had no financial training. He neglected to investigate the advisors background or what his qualifications were. Kareem's message is "trust, but verify." This will be addressed throughout the book.

I WON THE LOTTERY

If you are one of the 1% of the 1% who is lucky enough to get paid to play professionally in the sport you love, and hopefully paid well, then this section is for you. An article in the *Pacific Standard Magazine*, "How we set up our Professional Athletes to Fail", discusses the issues surrounding NBA's Keon Clark's fall from grace. Andy Billings, a professor from the University of Alabama comments that "we can't believe when a lottery winner runs out of money." While everyone sees the story and says "Well, that would never happen to me," the statistics show that the winner does not get any smarter with that sum of money. Just like a lottery winner, as an athlete you go from no money to an amount that seems unlimited very quickly. When you look at that formula, that's not just an athlete formula, that's a formula for disaster in EVERY walk of life, when all of a sudden someone enters a social class and a stratosphere they were unprepared for."

The stories are endless and I do not want this book to be a litany of athlete failures. I want to simply emphasize my reason for writing this book. I want to provide as much guidance to you, the young athlete; so that when you become an ex-athlete you will look back without the regrets of Kareem. Granted the saying that "youth is wasted on the young" will always be true and there will be "uh oh's" and disappointments and even some "I wish I hads" in life. However, with the help of this book, your advisors, your mentors, family and friends, you won't be the one who experiences financial disaster, as your high points and accomplishments will greatly outweigh them.

Forbes.com's online article, "Pro Athletes prove why you should stick to a financial playbook", states "As financial problems plague pro athletes, each headliner should serve as a reminder NOT to criticize, but to understand how these issues can take hold of our own financial lives. Playing by these fundamental rules and sticking to a SIMPLE financial playbook will help YOU avoid such a fate."

There are a few topics I will not be discussing in detail, but that are prevalent in the stories of athletes' financial disasters; Family, Children and Divorce.

CHILDREN AND DIVORCE

Plain and simple, the current cost to raise a normal child can be upwards of $235,000. The cost to raise the child of a professional athlete can cost upwards of $500,000 to $2,000,000 or more. Remember, you have to earn twice that amount before taxes to pay this cost over 18 years. You get it. The second issue that plagues athletes is divorce. Many times it's the transition that results in divorce, it may be that, just like your other friends and family, your spouse may not be ready to transition out of living the life of a professional athletes' spouse, or, the relationship cannot handle when you, the athlete, are suddenly home all the time. Transition creates stress in the relationship. You get it. Make sure you BOTH are ready for transition and BOTH are part of the discussion of spending, saving and budgeting.

FAMILY

"In developing a budget or a financial plan, we cannot forget the incredible strain that a sudden receipt of money means to the life of a person, athlete or not. Family inherently becomes one of the most significant sources of financial AND emotional stress. We have a need to help everyone. We want to give it away not only to those that helped us get to where we are, which may include parents or other family members, this is an immense amount of pressure to help friends and our community." GIVING requires planning! In a recent "Business Insider" article the "takeaway" is to remember to "make sure you can AFFORD to help others" before you do. Gifts or loans shouldn't come at the expenses of your own obligations, including saving for your own post career retirement. Also, be wary of giving money to people who are not taking steps to support themselves. You may want to help, but you could be making things worse." Your financial team should be willing and able to integrate your family as much as you want them to for financial education and understanding of what you CAN and CANNOT do. Think long term for everyone, not just for today.

CHAPTER 1: THE GAME PLAN

THE ANSWER TO "WHAT DO I DO NOW?"

A few years ago, a young man scheduled to undergo his third knee surgery, contacted us for help. While the doctors told him he could still play basketball recreationally, he knew his dream of "Going Pro" was over. At 20 years old, he was done. After 15 years of nothing but basketball, it was over in an instant. Although his college admission and scholarship were secured by his basketball skills, he still had the opportunity to finish college but without the sport and all he ever knew. He was lost and called our office with a very common phrase for many ex-athletes "What do I do now?"

The goal of this book is to provide you the necessary guidance when you reach your own "What do I do now?" moment, which often occurs when;

A high school athlete does not get a collegiate scholarship;

A college athlete does not get drafted;

A draft pick does not get signed;

A signed player gets cut;

Injury cccurs.

Let's face it: Retirement Happens, you will, one day, be an ex-athlete.

When hit with this often sudden and unexpected moment, this book's objective is for you to have no hesitation in answering that question. You will have a resource within these pages to resolve and answer the questions that you may not be currently prepared to answer. "What do I do now?" moments happen whether on or off a playing field; however, while well trained athletes are prepared to instantly react to sudden changes in the midst of play, often times there has been no training for off-the-field situations.

Preparation is the key to being able to respond immediately to any situation. Whether it is repetitive training and performance for participation in sports or solving life dilemmas, preparation helps answer the "What do I do now?" situation. In any sport, at any time, athletes face such sudden events as baseball line drives speeding straight towards them, football fumbles on goal lines, basketball rebounds, or stopping (or blocking) 100 mile per hour slap shots. In team competition, players must immediately understand and react to any given situation. For example, a football tight end must know how to execute his route without thinking, and a quarterback must be able to rapidly decide which receiver is open; a baseball pitcher must react swiftly to catch that ball hurtling towards his face. Such reactions and knowledge are attained through high level training and experience. Through training, you will develop muscle and play memory in order to immediately respond to the "What do I do now?" when it arises in the middle of a game.

As an athlete, you will prepare for a game through playbooks, film review and "walk throughs" to enable you to execute the plays in real time without hesitation. This book will help you as you develop your game plan and the thinking skills to respond to challenges "off the field," including final transition out of the sport you love. People agonize through difficulties because they have not prepared for a given situation's onset. For any situation, pre-planning – *preparation* – alleviates the stressful response to all of life's unexpected adversities. How may one prepare? This "playbook for preparation" answers that question.

Successful athletes understand basic values of training in their chosen sport. You know you need a supportive team to help you achieve your desired level of success. Be it coaches, trainers, or sports psychologists, a full team is critical for maintaining and sustaining your professional career.

The Three Legged Stool vs The Table

Consider a four-legged table and a three-legged stool. If one leg is removed from the table, that table is able to still stand, albeit a bit wobbly. However, if one leg is removed from the three-legged stool, the stool falls, as it must have all three legs to remain upright.

The same can be said in small business and is an absolute for any athlete. There are three "legs," that we will call The Professionals, which are critical to your professional structure to "remaining upright." Those three professionals are an attorney, investment advisor, and Certified Public Accountant.

You depend upon an attorney to deliver legal protection and advice. A common term used by everyone is "estate planning," which is a prime example of the importance of an attorney's services. The late Aretha Franklin died without preparing a will. Because of this oversight, approximately $30 million in legal fees and taxes will be taken from her estimated $80 million estate. A personal attorney is desirable for all legal matters one may encounter.

The second professional key to off the field and long term financial success is your investment advisor. Commonly they will have initials such as CFP or CLU. There are over 190 different "professional designations" which can be found at https://www.finra.org/investors/professional-designations. A prudent person depends upon a financial consultant to protect, maintain and grow the value of financial assets. The vehicles used to accomplish this may be life insurance, stocks, bonds, mutual funds, or annuities. It is critical that your investment advisor knows your short and long term financial goals. A wise professional athlete makes certain a reputable financial consultant is providing sound financial advice and asset supervision to maintain the athletes' monetary health.

The third professional is a Certified Public Accountant. Your business asset is your talent and most professional athlete's finances act like small businesses. Indispensable to you will be your CPA/business manager who will watch and manage your business and personal affairs from tax planning and return preparation to crucial business consultation. Many public tax preparers are IRS authorized, but do not understand the complex tax situations that plague professional athletes and many times will cause potential problems with the IRS. Having a CPA Certification is a key qualification for proper tax planning advice.

The same way the three legs are critical to support the stool, professional athletes need three strong supportive professionals to successfully support their business lives. Without strong legal, investment, and financial professionals, the athlete can risk being open to the common and public problems of fraud, misrepresentation, IRS Tax liens and possible jail time for errors of judgement.

Similar to the fact that all three legs must be in working order and that all members of the "coaching team" work together, it is imperative your professional advisors function together in your best interest. Teamwork is vital. You know full well the absolute necessity of teamwork on a playing field, a basketball court, or crammed in a bobsled. Just as selecting a coaching team, it is absolutely critical that you carefully choose the business team. Periodic team meetings in which all professionals and you gather to discuss the common "game plan" are excellent in keeping everyone involved on the same page, running the same direction on the same track, and planning the same game.

Planning? Yes! Game plans are essential to any sport. Financial plans are fundamental to any successful business. The question arises, "What is a plan?" A dictionary definition is "a system for achieving an objective; a method of doing something that is worked out in advance." Most certainly, that definition describes game plans which are systems for achieving objectives of winning games. Professional athletes are intimately familiar with and understand game plans; but what about financial or business plans? Sometimes, not so much.

Understanding both game and business plans is crucial for your future success. Such success results from a clear vision of anticipated goals. You must begin your journey into and out of your sport with clear goals in mind. All your actions with your professional team should be in line with the achievement of those goals. Meetings with your team are critical as you will be able to meet, discuss and alter your goals and objectives to meet the changing environment.

However, just as you do during a game, you must be flexible and work in an ever changing landscape. Injuries, trades, economic issues, as well as family life events and a multitude of other issues will create needed changes in your goals. At that point everything changes instantly and now you will be going to "Plan B."

What then? What of your plan? What about your Team? Is it still needed?

Unequivocally the answer is yes! You, professional athlete or not, need knowledge of legal matters such as living wills, investments in instruments such as 401Ks, and tax topics such as withholdings and refunds. For this knowledge you still need the support of experienced professionals I've mentioned: an attorney, an investment counselor, and a CPA. Building a personal relationship with these team members, as well as creating team rapport among all, becomes vitally important for the long run.

It takes a well-oiled machine, a closely working team to create a successful Game Plan. Your continued success towards your goals will depend upon skillful, superior, and trustworthy teamwork.

Success. According to the dictionary, "success" is several things. It is an "achievement of intention," "something that turns out well," or an "attainment of fame, wealth, or power." Normally, success is wonderful when an intention is achieved or something turns out for the good. Attainment of fame, wealth, or power is a positive accomplishment as well. Your on the field success breeds confidence in realizing intended athletic goals. It also can create a false confidence that success ON the field will spill over to success OFF the field. Highly successful professional athletes are vulnerable to pitfalls off the field without the proper level of advice and a strong support team.

You should be aware of these similar feelings of invincibility. The ability and confidence for a boxer to step into the ring can be an asset or a detriment outside of the ring. But as we discussed previously, while you're ON the field accomplishments take a team of trainers, coaches and teammates, your OFF the field without success also requires a strong team of professionals. Success may be short lived, a solid advisory team is not. Whether highly successful, somewhat successful or moderately successful, YOU will always triumph with such a team supporting your goals and objectives as they align with a healthy, productive business and life plan.

Confidence. Confidence exhibits deep strength, poise, and sureness. Confidence is modest. Confidence drives success. A person can be assuredly confident in their athletic accomplishments and an ego driven by assured self-confidence is one which delivers top achievements in sports performance, performing arts, or any profession. A highly successful professional athlete is one who has bedrock self-confidence in their abilities to positively perform functions of their particular sport and attain its highest objectives. You have the confidence necessary to perform at the highest level of your sport. But it is critical that you realize and truly understand that your capabilities ON the field may not translate into the same success OFF the field.

The important point to remember is that having experienced coaches greatly aid in navigating the changing landscape of life during and after the game. Some challenges are fundamental life issues while others are a complex matter of business, legal and investment decisions. We hope that you recognize the value of such guides, mentors, or experienced advisers and counselors.

Certainly, your attorney, investment advisor, and CPA are experienced advisers and indispensable to your support. They are essential foundations upon which a professional athlete's business management lies.

A mentor

In addition to the three professional advisors, it is important that you find a mentor. What is a mentor? Where does one find a mentor? Who is a mentor? The Dictionary defines a mentor as an experienced and trusted adviser. The knowledge, advice, and resources of a mentor depends on how you develop and build your relationship with your mentor. Your mentoring relationship is personal and unique to you. A mentor may share information with you about his or her own career path, as well as provide guidance, motivation, emotional support.

How to find a mentor? A mentor may be your family member, your father/mother, your aunt/uncle or sister/brother, it may also be a pastor or rabbi, a professor or coach, but it may also be someone you have not met yet. Networking is valuable in finding and building a relationship with a potential mentor. I will discuss more about networking later in this book, but it is important that you realize your brand value as an athlete and how to use it to your advantage to reach your goals. An easy start is as simple as attending functions of your college or team. Charity events that are sponsored by your team or college are easy ways to meet local business leaders. Professional association networking is particularly helpful in building portfolios of connections for professional athletes. Often athletes find mentors in coaches, trainers, owners, or family.

To recap, I hope that by reading this book you will begin to develop your own "game plan" that you, an established or soon-to-be successful professional, will recognize and appreciate that you cannot "go it alone" in negotiating pitfalls, potholes, and problems that will undoubtedly occur in your profession and personal life. Positive and profitable outcomes for both are significantly influenced by and greatly depend upon professional and personal support systems. As you prepare and follow game plans for participating in your sport, so should you prepare and follow the game plans for your business and life affairs. Using your three-professional team of an attorney, an investment advisor, and a CPA as well as developing a relationship with your mentor, you can successfully achieve your goals.

Takeaways, Questions and Actions:

1. Post Career – what do I want to do?
2. Make a list of whom do I know TODAY that can help me TOMORROW.
3. What do you think are your hurdles that will slow you down.
4. If I won the lottery, what would I do?

CHAPTER 2: NETWORKING AND BRANDING

NETWORKING, IT'S NOT WHAT YOU KNOW

In her book *Fit for Business*, Taylor Pak states that when she was recruited for college soccer, "you have limited time to show a coach who you are and what potential you have." "Trying to master your elevator speech at the age of 16 is difficult." However, she realized that the experience helped and guided her in realizing that she had already had many "job interviews."

> "It's fair to say that the recruiting process is equitable to the job search, which means that student athletes already have a great deal of practice. Finding the right home for your unique personality and skill set is not an easy task. It takes research (again lots of research) and some time to figure out what your strengths and weaknesses are."

As an athlete, you already have the tools and experience of the job interview. Taylor states that "it's OK to feel uncertainty and discomfort while thinking about the next chapter of your life because you have the OPPORTUNITY to make something of yourself."

There's an old saying in business that "it's not what you know but who you know," which holds very true in today's business environment.

Networking can make a huge difference in finding your post- athletic opportunities. Succeed or fail, it may also make the difference between surviving the three-year transition out of athletics or not; the difference of finding the job or position that you want or not. In interviews with my clients who are former professional athletes, all of them told me that it's very difficult to transition out of athletics. My experience is that it takes approximately three years to make that transition. Some may be shorter and some may be longer. I use the term athletics and not PROFESSIONAL athletics as there are struggles in both the post collegiate world (called "post-graduate depression") as well as transitioning from professional athletics. The issue being that you are no longer identified as an athlete. As a student athlete at the age of 20, you have been playing your sport for perhaps over 15 years.

You may be able to transition out of athletics when you complete college, straight into a job. You may be able to transition out of athletics after playing professional sports for 10 years as well, but there is still a transition period when you are no longer on a team mandated schedule where you are being told where, what and when. You are now completely on your own. It is very difficult when the time ends as an athlete. As a collegiate athlete, you are no longer on a schedule being told when to eat, sleep, study, practice, play, be there, and be here. In addition to the scheduled life you are used to, there is one more big change when you transition out of the professional world, MONEY. There comes a time in EVERY professional athlete's life when the money stops and your support group, the people that you've been around for years, is no longer there. Your attorney will still be involved with your changing estate planning needs, your CPA will still be involved with your business and your taxes. However, many of your now former teammates may be having their own issues or maybe they're still playing and you are no longer part of that club.

Now what do I do?

When that moment hits and you realize that you are no longer a collegiate or professional athlete that is when all your prior NETWORKING efforts come into play. I cannot stress the importance of networking. What is networking? Networking is connecting with other people in business, industries or professions that are of interest to you. It also involves meeting people who might be able to help you in the future. When I talked about "it's not what you know but who you know," that is the key to networking.

Harvey MacKay, a well-known syndicated columnist, author and business networking guru, talks about knowing your clients and how critical that knowledge is to be able to grow and maintain a business. It's the same way for a student-athlete or a professional athlete, with one exception. As an athlete, you may have the ability to get your "foot in the door" where others cannot. For instance, as a member of a collegiate athletic team, you have an opportunity to interact with alumni and boosters, all of whom may be successful businesses people in the community. When attending charity events, it's important that you "kick butt and take names." More importantly, keep the information of whom you met. You may want to have somebody help you follow up after meetings through email, calling or setting up a lunch. Meeting those contacts can be beneficial, especially if they can help you with a project or a business in which you are interested. Take advantage of the opportunities presented to you.

Wayne Kimmel, in his book *Six Degrees of Wayne Kimmel,* the networking guru and venture capitalist at Seventy Six Capital has "the Gospel" for networking.

> "How do you meet the people that will become your most trusted and influential relationships? You have to go out and find them. You never know who (sic) they're going to be, so you have to cast as wide a net as possible."

Networking as a professional athlete is much different than as a student athlete. There are more opportunities for you to get out into the community and meet the people that are going to help you when you are an ex-athlete or former player.

There are two things to remember in networking. First, the "never say no" attitude. Remember Kareem's advice to get out there and "engage?" While you don't want to overdo your schedule, you never know what new opportunities will come from attending an event. The other is "don't worry about what people want FROM you," instead flip it and look at it as "what can they do FOR you." You do not realize that you have the power to meet anyone. I am sure that if LeBron James wanted to meet the president of any fortune 100 company, Microsoft, Uber, Amazon it would only take one phone call. While you may not be LeBron, you still have a great opportunity to meet people in your community. If you play on a minor league team, a smaller town may still offer you opportunities to meet with local business leaders and talk with them about what you want to do in the future.

Create your contact list, what used to be known as a Rolodex. While many of you are being taught how to use LinkedIn, note that, unlike Instagram, it is not a goal to have a million connections. Instead, you want to try and make your contacts fewer but more important. Quality vs Quantity. You are better off knowing 20 people really well than having over 500 contacts that you barely know.

Examples of the two ideas from above are from two former Arizona Cardinals players. First, John Bronson tells the story of his "never say no" experience. Once one of his teammates called him to say he wasn't able to go the (then called) Phoenix Open golf tournament and wanted to know if John would fill in for him. "Sure," he said without knowing exactly what he was doing. As it turned out, John was going to be a "celebrity" caddy for the Pro-AM. John spent the next 8 hours as a celebrity caddy talking to Jimmy Walker, a local, well known and very well connected investment advisor. Mr. Walker happens to also host a very significant charity event for the Mohammed Ali Foundation for Parkinson's Disease. The event is called "Fight Night," and it's a high-ranking social event. He invited John to attend. John said he went to the event feeling like "a big man in town" because he was an Arizona Cardinals player and was invited to this major event. He was a celebrity. When he walked in, however, he found himself in the middle of A-listers from hollywood, politics, and business. It was at this event that John will tell you that he met his best friend and long-time mentor and business advisor. Never say no.

John Skelton, another former Arizona Cardinals player, had a different lesson. In preparing this book, I asked him, "What are the things that you wished you would have done when you were playing?" He said that as an athlete he was always cautious when at an event. He was wary of what people wanted FROM him. Because, as an athlete, you are trained to be wary of people taking advantage of you, he said he would put up a wall to guard against that risk. In hindsight, John said he wished he would have approached the events completely differently, with the view of "what can you do FOR me." He now realizes that he could have received valuable contacts in the business world if he had been open to networking with people instead of closing them off. All of this "connecting" does not mean that you should be open to everyone without properly vetting a new contact; you should always make sure to have a member of your trusted advisory team to help you do that. You might even perhaps take a "wingman" that can help you "work the room."

Much like in the dating world and being at a party, everyone at the event knows why they are there. It may be drinks or cigars at a bar or restaurant; playing golf; attending a charity event or sometimes just being open to new contacts when you are doing your normal day to day activities. All colleges and sports teams sponsor charity events that you may, as a member of the team, be required to attend.

Community and business leaders are most of the attendees at these events and it's a great opportunity for you to meet people who might be able to help you transition from your "sporting world" to the "regular world" when that time comes. I urge you to get comfortable and be open to every opportunity you have and build your network of meaningful contacts.

Your meaningful contacts are people you know something about. They are not just a connection you made by clicking "Accept." You may know about their jobs, what they actually do, their birthdays or family members; you may have some common business acquaintances. The longer you are in business, the more you network, the more your contacts may become your friends as well.

A good example of this is a business networking event I attended. At the meeting there was an Arizona Cardinal's player, who was on injured reserve. He was sitting with the other Cardinals players and not meeting with the business people who also attended the event. I mentioned to him, "You realize that everybody in this room is afraid to come up and talk to you?" He said, "What do you mean?" I told him, "I understand you're on injured reserve, but you play in the NFL. You realize that everybody in this room would love to just chat with you. You have an opportunity to meet all these business people. Take advantage of it."

Every chance you have, get the contact information. Show interest in what they're about. Do not be surprised, they will be far more interested in YOUR stories of being an athlete. Build your networking file. Follow up with people you've met. Go to events. Develop real friendships with people outside of your athletic world. Grow your support system. As a professional athlete, you have a wonderful opportunity to network.

> More gospel from Wayne: "there will be nights when you would rather hangout with your family and friends instead of going to a networking, political or charity event. GO ANYWAY. You never know who you will meet. This is a long game. Building relationships is like a marathon, not a sprint."

Building Brand Value

In addition to growing your post career portfolio, it is important that you show who you are TODAY. Who are you and what is your BRAND.

First, what is branding? Simply put, in the retail world, a brand is something that identifies a product or an idea in people's minds. For example, "Kleenex" conjures up a small paper tissue in people's minds whether or not that tissue is a Kleenex brand tissue, Puff, or Angel Soft. If you sneezed, you probably would say to me, "Hand me a Kleenex, please." I doubt if you would ask me to hand you a facial tissue. Other common, successful retail brands include Saran Wrap and Band Aids and hundreds of other household names.

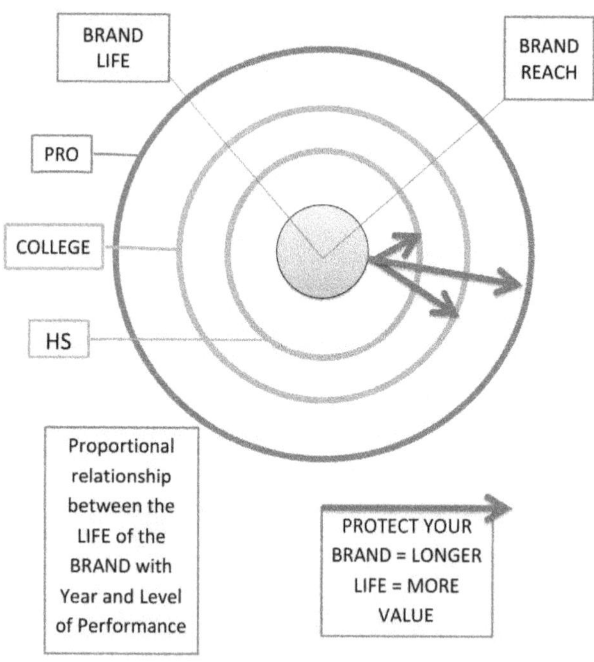

This figure illustrates brand life for the athlete. Brand life or Brand Value have both a geographical (local, state, national or international) reach as well as a time factor or "life" to it.

A name like "Michael Jordan" has a brand value that has a worldwide geographic reach and probably has a brand life value that will last for quite some time. While you might not be Michael Jordan, Wayne Gretzky, Joe Montana or Derek Jeter, you do have Brand Value if you play professional sports, and in some cases you have brand value if you play collegiate sports (otherwise you might not be getting a scholarship.)

When you are on a professional team, you have an automatic brand by just being on that team. You are a Green Bay Packer, a Chicago Bull, a Los Angeles Dodger, or a Vegas Golden Night. Additionally, you have the ability to build that brand value while you are playing so that it has longevity and prominence after you are retired from sports.

Branding and Philanthropy

One of the most common ways an athlete can create a brand is through charitable work. Because, as when we talk about media misconceptions, we discuss that the GOOD stories can gain media attention and build brand value. College and professional teams are always involved in the community. You have a jump start and are probably already doing some work within the community through your team. Successful athletes can bring a strong brand value and influence to a charity, thereby securing the brand value of the athlete. Having your name and likeness out in the community can be one of the strongest assets you bring to an employer, team, college or endorsement sponsor. As we talk about your name and likeness, let's try to look at what a BRAND is and how you can create, grow, maintain and monetize your BRAND.

You can have a brand that represents you off the court and a separate one that represents you on the court. While your "on the field" brand is really based on how you play the game, your "off the field" brand is based on your outside activities, community involvement, being a voice of the team or your sport, and even how you represent yourself online.

Basically, your brand is how people see you, hear you; your mission and your value and your image. WHY DO I CARE how people see me? Well if you have aspirations to create income from your on the field opportunities, YOU SHOULD CARE. For example, what kind of "brand" do you think of when you think of Larry Fitzgerald? You "know" them by their brands.

UNFORTUNATELY, in today's world, what you portray to people is how others see you. Don't forget by "others" I mean to include future coaches, general managers, employers as well as the general public. Perception is reality. You create your own brand in their minds, and that is how you can FAIL or SUCCEED in creating a brand. Now you might read this and say "I don't care." And that's OK. You do NOT have to create a brand, market a brand and monetize a brand. This chapter may not be relevant to you.

However, whether you like it or not, you are being judged by the impression you leave on others and the impression you make on social media. When a prospective college, professional team or other employer looks at you as a candidate, they currently have staff that will search social media to see if there is ANY dirt on you. Trust me I do the same when I look to hire a new staff member.

This is especially true with Social Media! If you portray yourself as a wild partygoer on Instagram, people may see you as immature and irresponsible. If they see you attending charity events, they may see you as a responsible community leader. Whatever image you put out on Social Media can, for better or worse, become your brand. You want to be extremely careful how you brand yourself on Social Media because once you put something on the Web it never goes away.

Which of those items from your past would you want shown to the public, your potential team coach/GM or to your possible employer? Whatever you put on Social Media, you put on your resume. However you portray yourself on Social Media is how you build your brand. Build your brand thoughtfully. Build your brand carefully. Build your brand effectively for the best results for you.

You can use Social Media to your advantage to develop a mature, reliable, and sensible brand for yourself, or you can irresponsibly create a foolish, immature, and unreliable brand. You can use Social Media to build your brand as a dependable and levelheaded person or you can damage your future. It's up to you. What type of person do you want people to see you as? How do you want to be branded?

Network and Branding go hand-in-hand. As you network with people, you also build your brand in their eyes. Whether you're networking in person with others at a social event or sitting at a computer posting on Social Media, you're building your brand. Step outside of yourself and look at you through other people's eyes. What do they see at a business meeting or social gathering? What kind of impression do they get about you from your Instagram posts or

Twitter feed? The answers to those questions are up to you. You are the writer of your life's story. You are the builder of your brand. Get out there and network! With every hand you shake and with every post you post, build your fine, strong, outstanding brand!

- Networking Tips
    - Get out there
    - Follow Up
    - Don't be shy
    - Get Help

- Branding Ideas
    - Find your own identity.
    - What do you stand for?
    - Mind your Mission Statement.
    - Donor Advised Funds.

Takeaways, Questions and Actions:

1. What is my brand on the field?
2. What do I want my brand to be off the field?
3. Who can help me network if I am uncomfortable?
4. List 3 events I can attend.
5. List 3 business contacts I know and can reach out to.
6. List 3 business contacts I WANT to talk to and who can help me connect.

CHAPTER 3: DEALING WITH MEDIA MISCOMMUNICATIONS

In her book *Fit for Business*, Taylor Pak discussed the public service announcement that the NCAA produced for television: "There are over 400,000 NCAA student-athletes and just about all of us will be going pro in something other than sports" (NCAA 2011). In fact, barely 1% of NCAA athletes will "go pro," while most will transition into regular jobs and professions. The message was meant to dispel the "dumb jock" stereotype. However, although the media still portrays the "dumb jock" stereotype in film and television, such media portrayals do not need to be the norm. Sensationalism sells and the tide is changing as more athletes are using the media to show their successes.

Media coverage can be a challenge for you as an athlete, especially as it relates to your finances. As an athlete, you are a magnet for the media. If you make unwise financial decisions and lose money, you are really a wonderful target for the media.

All you have to do is Google "Athlete Financial Disasters" to find a story on every single time an athlete made a financially poor decision, was defrauded or just plain "went broke" In ESPN film's 30 for 30 movie "Broke", we saw athletes sweating under the lights explaining how they wish they would have done things differently or how they trusted the wrong people.

You must be careful in your investment choices. The stories of athletes who were defrauded, stolen from, made poor business decisions or just plain over spent date back decades, to the 1930's and 1940's. Sometimes athletes with good advisors or who were doing well made one or two bad choices unintentionally. Athletes, like San Francisco Giants' pitcher Jake Peavy, Denver Broncos' quarterback Mark Sanchez, and former MLB pitcher Roy Oswalt lost millions of dollars in an alleged Ponzi like fraud and the media put them in an unwanted spotlight as a result.

Ponzi Schemes are illegal, and among the most difficult to detect methods of fraud. They promise investors large returns with little or no risk of losing money. Early investors pay their money to an operator, and, as more investors pay in, the operator pays back early investors with late investors' money. A Ponzi scheme requires an initial investment with promises of above-average returns. The scheme is named after a 1920s Boston businessman, Charles Ponzi, who became infamous for using the technique. Ash Narayan, as a board member of The Ticket Reserve Company and financial advisor to many professional athletes defrauded Peavy, Sanchez and Oswalt (source USA Today) (https://www.sec.gov/litigation/admin/2017/34-79991.pdf) All three said they trusted Narayan because he said he was a CPA and a Christian and represented other professional athletes. It turns out he was not a CPA, which could have been easily verified through the AICPA (American Institute of Certified Public Accountants) as we discuss in the "Creating the Team" chapter.

A media challenge many athletes have faced is that the public interpret those media reports as pro athletes being "dumb jocks." A typical negative reaction to such media reports might go like this: "Athletes shouldn't be paid all this money because they just do stupid stuff with it." You may face this challenge as well. You could be fighting the perception of being a "dumb jock," and you know very well you're not! You just need some professional help and support regarding your finances and investments.

Media coverage can "miscommunicate" by generating misconceptions about people, especially successful professional athletes. It is not that the media report itself is negative but that the media merely reports what has happened. In this case, a financial failure. However, those reports are often misinterpreted or miscommunicated when people see a well-paid athlete in financial difficulty.

Nevertheless, such "media miscommunications" can also offer an opportunity for people to want to help athletes in financial trouble. I am writing this book to give you help in making wise financial decisions. I want to help you safely navigate the minefield of potential financial disasters.

You are not alone in needing help. Foolish financial mistakes happen. Many well-educated, professionals like lawyers, doctors, and wealthy business people were fooled and lost money in the Bernie Madoff Ponzi Scheme, for example. Bernie Madoff, a formerly well-respected member of the financial industry, cheated his clients out of a total of $65 billion. In 2009 he was sentenced to 150 years in federal prison and ordered to pay billions in repayments and restitution. Madoff ran a very intricate scheme that fooled a lot of professional people who should have known better. The story of Bernie Madoff and his clients who lost millions of dollars was a very big media story which put many people in the spotlight.

Your team of professional advisors are able to offer you a "different sets of eyes" to see if it makes sense for your situation.

How do you find them? There are many ways to research and verify that people have licenses and expertise they say they have. If you're looking for a Certified Public Accountant, contact the AICPA, the American Institute of Certified Public Accountants. In addition, each state has a state board of accountancy. For an attorney, you can contact your state's bar association. For an Investment Advisor, you can contact FINRA, the Financial Industry Regulatory Authority, and check their website called www.brokercheck.com. Type in the broker's name, and you can find all you need to know about their licensing, employment and any complaints or licensing problems.

You still want to do additional "due diligence" in researching your financial team before you hire them. "Due Diligence" is defined as "the care a reasonable person exercises to avoid harm to their property." It is the research you do in advance as you build your advisory team, invest, or make a business deal. It is making sure to the best of your ability that the financial decisions you make with your financial team are ones that will help you and not hurt you.

Besides reporting financial failures, media also reports financial successes such as Roger Staubach (Real Estate), John Elway (Restauranteur), Magic Johnson (Business), as well as those with strong philanthropic endeavors (Mia Hamm, Jeff Gordon, Warren Dunn, Andre Agasi, Doug Flutie). Sometimes such reporting of successes can make an athlete's ego say "I'm a great athlete in my sport, so I must be a great business person as well." You must be careful not to fall into this trap. Media reporting of financial successes can be both negative and positive. While reporting of failures can scare you into not trusting anybody because you don't want to wind up like other athletes went "Broke", reporting of successes can make you think: "If John Elway can open up a chain of restaurants, so can I!" Not exactly true. You have to be objective in your financial dealings. You have to make sure you have the best expert advice, and that you are in line with your financial goals. You have your own unique gifts, talents, and financial needs.

I mentioned earlier in this chapter that you want checks and balances for your monetary system so you can manage your finances properly with your financial advisory team. You want to understand how your money works, when and how it's invested, and how banking works. You want to understand your checking accounts as well as other different types of accounts to help with checks and balances of your money. You want to understand banks and banking regulations. You want to know what banks can do and what they can't do for you. I will cover this in the next chapter.

Takeaways, Questions and Actions:

1. Find someone with experience from whom you can learn.
2. Find 3 failures and find out "what went wrong" (discuss with my advisors).
3. Find 3 success stories and find out "what went right"(discuss with my advisors).

CHAPTER 4: MONEY AND BANKING

Two interconnected financial errors that can drastically affect your money are overspending and falling into debt. In the game, athletes face certain risks on the field — for example, the possibility of getting injured during a game or facing penalties for illegal plays. (VISA Financial Soccer)

Yet, simple actions like warming up before hitting the field and knowing the rules of the game can help minimize the possibility of either scenario. Likewise, certain actions and oversights can negatively impact your personal finances. For example, adopting bad habits like buying items on credit that you can't really afford and failing to create a budget can easily lead to accumulating unwanted debt. Living beyond your means and buying more WANTS than you can afford, impulse buying and other bad money habits can, in the long run, destroy your financial wellbeing.

Debt is when you owe money. Debt is not a bad thing, but you have to be careful not to accumulate more than you can afford to pay back. One way to get into debt is to make impulsive spending decisions without considering whether or not you can afford or really need something.

In this chapter I want to talk about money. There is a common saying that "Money makes the world go 'round." Money is what we want more of when we work; it allows us to pay for stuff; pay for food, do charitable work, have fun.

Plain and simple, let's be honest, we all want to obtain enough wealth to accomplish our goals and dreams, but we also want to spend it wisely. Since you probably don't walk around with all of your cash in a duffel bag like Floyd Mayweather, it's important that you understand what money really is and how it works.

Money and banking are almost inseparable. Issues with money and banking can be complicated, and that is why you need the three professional financial advisors on your team. What is money? It is a medium of legal exchange used to measure the value of goods and services. In today's world money consists of gold, silver, or coins and paper. In ancient Rome salt was used as money. The Roman government paid their army and government workers with measures of salt because salt was an extremely valuable commodity. In fact, our word "salary" stems from the Roman word "salarium," meaning "salt money."

What happens to money when you earn it? If you are smart, you put it in a bank. Thus, it's very important that you understand your relationship with your bank.

A bank is defined as "a business that keeps money for individual people or companies, exchanges currencies, makes loans, and offers other financial services." It's easy to think that you merely deposit your money in your bank and it sits there for you to withdraw it when you need it. That is not the way banks work. The primary function of any bank is to use money deposited by you and others to lend out for other people to buy real estate, start and grow businesses, improve homes, buy cars, or pay for college tuition, just to name a few. When you deposit your money, it goes into a big pool of money with all the other customers making deposits.

The Bank may give you 1% or 2% interest on your money. Meanwhile, they take that money and they loan it out to somebody else to buy a house, a car or even to start a business. On that loan they charge them a larger interest rate and the bank makes money based on the difference between the two interest rates. Example; they may pay you 2% and they may charge somebody else 8%; they use that 6% difference to run the bank and make a profit.

Banks move money into the economy by making loans and being paid back with interest. Part of your money, along with other depositors' money, is always moving through society and helping the economy.

Since you don't carry around your cash in a bag, you can have access to your cash through an ATM, going to the bank or just using a credit or debit card to spend the money that you have. When we talk about saving money the most important thing is to understand how you earn it first. If you don't know WHEN your money is coming or WHERE it is coming from, you can't possibly plan wisely for when and what to spend.

Show me the Money

When will you get paid? Well, that depends. You may have a guaranteed contract or you may not. You may get paid only during the season or you may get paid evenly throughout the year like a "regular" job. NFL players get paid 8 times a year during the season, thus all their money is split into those few paychecks. That's why it's critical for NFL players to budget. Because they only get paid from September to December they have to live from January until the next paycheck in September. Planning is critical.

What is planning for spending? It is called a budget. Everybody hates the word budget so I just say to my clients "we are going to set up your savings and spending plan". It's important that you sit down with your CPA/business manager to discuss what your goals are and that includes goals for savings and perhaps goals for spending. There may be things that you want to buy that you have been waiting for and that's okay, just plan for it.

When I work with players I try not to dig into every single item that might be spent every day. For instance, how much is your cable bill? or how much is your cell phone bill? We really try to look at what is your "MONTHLY NUT" of spending, how much you have left over to save and how to control the spending. When you're earning a very high income, you have to look at things much differently than when you are out of sports and just earning a regular wage or living on retirement income. At that point you really do have to look at every single little dime that goes out to make sure that you're not spending $400 on a cable bill that you really can't afford.

Working on a budget is critical from day one before you get the money from your first paycheck. Sit down and figure out what you can spend and what you must save. Don't forget, you also have to save for taxes and you have to save for your retirement as well. Since no one knows whether their career will be one day, one year, one decade or longer, make sure to plan conservatively for the TRANSITION when you're done.

Articles in the media discuss how 78% of athletes "go broke" or have financial issues within three years after their playing career is over. When you are done playing the most difficult time is the transition to reality. Many people who exit the military after 20 years of service have the same issue of going back to civilian life. Financial issues are not always because of someone doing something wrong, it is more likely just a poorly executed transition plan. An investment advisor friend of mine says "Failing to plan, is planning to fail."

It is scary to realize the inevitable fact that a time will come when you will never play again. It may be counterproductive to dwell on this in the middle of the season, but that doesn't mean you shouldn't plan for it. Every athlete will be a former athlete whether it's one day, one month, one year or one decade away, and planning for that day is critical. That is what this book is all about.

In developing a budget and spending plan, you have to realize that you have different types of expenses. They can be described in different ways, but I like to use simple terms, Needs and Wants.

Your needs are all of the monthly expenses associated with essential goods and services that keep your life stable. A need is something you must have, like rent, food, telephone, clothing, utilities, basically a roof above your head, food on your plate and clothes on your back.

Now, if you ask a 14 year old that's a different answer, like "I NEED that X Box360." Youthful ignorance.

Wants are discretionary things or choices you can live without, but you really want. Wants are goods and services that are not essential to daily living, but they are often things that make people happy or may make life seem a little easier or more special.

Those items might include an expensive house or apartment, a $1,200 jacket, $900 shoes, or a $100,000 car. It is important to look at every single purchase as "do I NEED this or do I merely WANT this?" I ask my children the same question, "is this a NEED or a WANT?"

To go a little further, some of your expenses are "fixed", which means they are the same each month. One example is rent or your mortgage. Other expenses are "variable." These include utilities, medical bills, car repairs or other items that change with the given situation.

Planning how to control your expenses and savings is how you make a budget. A budget could be compared to a savings plan. Once you know how much your monthly expenses are, you want to be sure to save enough money from every paycheck to be certain all fixed expenses are covered. You can set a goal as to how much total money you want to have saved at year's end, so you want to be sure you set aside a certain amount from each paycheck which will total your goal at year's end. If you are a professional athlete and want to have $120,000.00 saved by year's end, then your budget would include saving $10,000.00 per month. After you have saved for your fixed expenses and your savings, what is left is your discretionary money to be spent however you like on the "wants." With my clients, I will sometimes create special accounts for large expenditures. We may have a "house account" to save for a house or a tax account to make sure we save and account for taxes.

Credit

Part of the money process is understanding credit, why it is important and how it relates to your money. Credit is defined as "an arrangement by which a buyer can take possession of something now and pay for it over a period of time." Credit involves two people, the LENDER and the BORROWER. You are the borrower and the bank (credit card company) is the LENDER.

Credit allows you the flexibility to spend and to schedule when your payment is due, which is called CASH FLOW MANAGEMENT. In addition everyone loves to earn cash back and mileage rewards.

NOW is the time to start getting into the conversation of credit and using your money wisely.

Credit can help if you need money for emergencies such as illness, accidents, or unexpected expenses. Credit can also function as a way to pay for necessities such as groceries, gasoline, or car repairs. Credit can also hurt you if you spend more than you can repay.

Credit is borrowed money, pure and simple. You agree to pay back the amount you borrowed plus interest and finance charges. Interest and finance charges add up quickly. People often get themselves into financial trouble when their debt payments outweigh their income. You want to be sure you are always able to keep up with your payments on your credit cards. Credit cards are a fast and convenient way to borrow and spend money, which makes them one of the easiest ways to get into debt trouble.

Your financial health is often expressed by one number – your Credit Score. Your Credit Score is the REPORT CARD of your credit. It shows lenders how responsibly you have managed loans, lines of credit, and your financial obligations over a period of time. Your credit history is a record of your credit life and how well you manage money. Most importantly your credit score stays with you FOREVER. If you make any mistake, somethings as simple as moving and forgetting to pay a credit card for 2 months or not paying your final water/electric bill, you may not be able to remove that error for SEVEN years. So if you make a mistake in college, it may stay with you until you are 30. If you think a small issue like going to collections for a $120.00 medical bill or utility bill won't hurt you, think again. It can be the difference between being able to rent an apartment or not. YES, prospective apartment landlords will check your credit; prospective employers will check your credit. It is a way to gauge how fiscally responsible you are, whether you like it or not.

Additionally, a good credit score is necessary to make major purchase such as a car or a house or to get the BLACK CENTURION CARD.

The Mystery of your Credit Report

We have all seen the commercials for Credit Karma or for the "free credit scores." Those commercials are not being shown to sell you something but to warn you about ignoring your credit. Your credit score can change almost daily, whenever there are any changes to your credit including balance on a card, late payments, "running" your credit for a car loan, apartment or house loan, even in the store when you get a discount for "opening a credit card" with that store. Credit scores are affected by Payment History, Amounts Owed, Length of Credit History, Types of Credit Used, and New Credit.

Your payment history represents up to 40% of your overall rating:

- The number of loan and credit accounts you have paid on time.
- The number of accounts you are currently at least 30 days behind payment.
- If you have been bankrupt or had accounts sent to collections.
- How many days any delinquent accounts are past due.
- Dollar amounts past due or sent to collections.

If you have failed to make payments as agreed with your lender, your credit score will show that.

What you owe accounts for at least 30% of your credit score. It indicates if you are likely to face serious financial problems in the future. This part of your score is based upon:

- The number of accounts that carry a balance.
- How much credit you use every month. It is extremely important that you do not "Max Out" your cards.
- How much you owe on existing credit cards or loans.

New credit reflects your recent financial activity and predicts how you will behave with your credit in the future. It includes:

- How many loans or new credit cards you have opened in recent months.
- How long it's been since you opened your newest account.

- The number of times you've applied for credit in the past 12 months. (Sometimes called a "hard pull.")
- How long it has been since your last credit inquiry.

It is good to monitor your credit score just like the commercials on TV say you should. There are three major credit reporting agencies – Equifax, Experian, and TransUnion. You can get your score for free online, or you can subscribe for monthly monitoring, which, in today's world of identity theft can be extremely useful.

A good credit standing also extends beyond purchases because your credit information may be used by potential employers and landlords as part of approving you or denying you. As mentioned previously, credit is not only the borrowing of money on a credit card; it is also your financial status and reputation.

There are four types of credit:

Revolving Credit - (like a Southwest Airlines Visa Card) A bank will give you a card with a maximum credit limit and you can only make charges up to that limit. Each month you can pay off the full balance, however, if you don't pay off the balance in full, you will need to make a minimum payment, which will include interest/finance charges. You can improve and build your credit score as you use and pay your charges. Most credit cards are of this type, but they are also the ones that get you in trouble the fastest.

Charge Cards - (like the Centurion/Black card from American Express)– You can use charge cards the same way you use a Revolving Credit card, but you must pay the total balance due every month.

Service Credit - These are your service providers: utility company for electricity, phone company, gym memberships, water bill, etc. You receive a monthly bill for services provided. If you have bad credit you may have to give them a deposit to secure your account.

Installment credit - Car loans and house mortgages are two good examples of installment credit. You receive a loan for a certain amount of money and you must repay that loan with a regular (fixed or variable) monthly payment, plus interest, over a certain period of time.

Finally, there are two categories of credit: secured and unsecured. Secured credit is a loan backed by an asset or collateral, such as your home or your car. Unsecured credit is a loan with no collateral, like credit cards, medical bills, service bills, and student loans.

Why is it helpful to have good credit? Credit is how lenders view who you are and what kind of financially responsible borrower you are. If you have always paid with cash, you actually have no credit history at all. Having no credit history can make lenders wary of you. No credit history can make you the "odd person out" in society. It may seem backwards, but no credit history can be as negative as bad credit history.

If you don't have credit now, it would be a wise idea to develop a good credit history. This can be difficult because it's the "catch 22." No one will give you credit unless you have a credit score, but you cannot get your credit score without credit. Sometimes the best way is to start with a low balance credit card. If you are under 21, you may have to find a student credit card. Once you have a job and are earning income, you can try to get a car loan. Keep your payments steady and up-to-date. Pay off your credit cards. Be responsible and credit wise.

Now that we have talked about budgets and credit, we can talk about how both affect the two likely biggest purchases of your life, your car and your house. Let's say you wish to buy a house. Obviously, you need to ask yourself how much house can I afford. You must realize that money spent on a house requires a lot more than just paying the mortgage. There are utility and maintenance bills, property taxes, and homeowner's insurance requirements as well. A basic mortgage number can quickly escalate with additional fees. Upkeep can be more than your mortgage. The maintenance on a 5,000 square foot house on an acre of land can be as much as $5,000 per month. The bigger the house the higher the maintenance bills will be. (See Appendix XX for the list and complications of buying a home or car.)

Thanks to MTV Cribs, houses have become physical representations of a person's wealth and success. They can also be representations of a person's personality in a way that showcases how they want to be perceived. Beware of such thinking.

TRANSITION LESSONS
Money and Credit

Spending especially becomes an issue when you retire, become injured, ill or are released.

The time of TRANSITION is the primary focus of this book, which aims to prepare you for TRANSITION from athletics to civilian life.

How it happens is irrelevant. The important point will be the time you no longer have the income. Think of it as driving on a freeway at 75 miles per hour. You're zipping along just fine. A sudden stop, a sudden slam on the breaks and watch out. The faster you are going, the longer it takes to slow down.

You will need to slam on the spending breaks when your career ends. If you are not properly prepared for the drop in your income, you will become one of the statistics. Studies have shown that 78% of athletes have post-career financial problems. Anything you can do to train yourself to be aware of your upcoming spending slowdown will greatly help you when it's actually time to slow down. You want to spend wisely now as you prepare yourself.

CHAPTER 5: PLANNING FOR YOUR FINANCIAL FUTURE

A Look at Risk Management

How do you prepare for the day of post career retirement? How do you plan for your financial future when your stream of income changes? A good way to do this is through investing your present money with financial strategies that will match with your future anticipated needs whether it is income or growth of value for the future.

Strategies include investing in stocks and bonds, (which can be mutual funds, exchange-traded funds, or similar related investments.) It can be as simple as a savings plan while you play. Keeping money in cash is not a bad idea if you cannot afford the risk of your investments going down in value, rather you cannot afford the time to wait for it to recover.

Other investments may include real estate or even more exotic investments like precious metals (gold/silver), private equity funds, jewelry, cars, or artwork.

A "dictionary definition" of investing is "the act of committing money or capital to an endeavor with the expectation of obtaining an additional income or profit." Renowned investor Warren Buffett simply defines investing as "the process of laying out money now to receive more money in the future."

There are always risks in investing. The value of stocks and bonds fluctuate on a daily basis. Real estate can decrease in value with changes in the market. There are always inherent risks of your investment losing money in the future.

Everyday life is filled with risks. But in some cases, you can purchase insurance to protect you from the risk. Homeowners insurance, for instance, will protect you if your house catches fire, or auto insurance in the case of an auto accident.

While there is no insurance policy against losing the value of investments, you can manage your risks through proper planning.

What is "risk?"

It is a chance of something going wrong. For health insurance, it is a risk the health insurance company takes that you will get sick or injured. In car insurance, it is the risk that your auto insurance company takes that your car will be damaged. In homeowners insurance, it is a risk of fire or that a tree will fall on your house during a storm. In investing, it is the possibility you will lose the value of your investments.

"The bigger risk, the bigger reward"

Most sports have high risk levels of injuries, but they also have a high reward in the level of compensation to athletes. Arizona Cardinal Larry Fitzgerald's 2018 salary was $11 million. LeBron James of the Los Angeles Lakers 2018 salary was $35.65 million. Seattle Seahawks' quarterback Russell Wilson presently has career earnings of $74.36 million over seven seasons. High risks and high rewards.

What is your willingness to accept RISK? It is determining your level of tolerance, your "acceptable" risk related to your investments. It can be low, high, or middle, and anywhere on a scale from 1 to 10.

Understanding what risk tolerance means is important before you consider investing. Perhaps you invest $50,000 in stocks and your $50,000 falls to $10,000. Do you have the ability to be "ok" with that drop in investment, knowing that it may recover or it may not and you may have to reevaluate your investment strategy? Can you afford a PERMANENT loss of that one investment?

Risk levels can be divided into four categories from highest risk to lowest risk, as follows:

- Speculative – junk bonds, collectibles, options, futures
- Growth – real estate, mutual funds, variable annuities
- Income – corporate bonds, preferred stock, treasury or government bonds
- Savings – cash, savings bonds, fixed annuities, money market accounts

To understand the complexities of each of the above investments is not the critical point here. What is essential is that you have a basic understanding that every investment has some risk, and understand that there are different levels of risk associated with each investment. These are discussions that should be had with your advisors over and over until you understand "where's my money, dude" as Kareem mentioned. Mutual funds are a common type of investment. They allow the investor to share in the expertise of the fund manager to pick and choose stocks and bonds within the fund. The mutual fund collects investment dollars from many investors for the purpose of investing in stocks, bonds or other assets depending on the "fund." There can be stock funds, bond funds, gold funds and a host of other investment portfolio choices. While mutual funds allow you to determine a specific level of risk based on the type of fund you choose, your return, just like the stock market, is not guaranteed. In addition, mutual funds can be subject to management fees that create a high cost to own.

As I am NOT an investment advisor, I will not be giving you a full explanation of different investments but I will try to give you an overview of Stocks and Bonds. Let's look at bonds first.

When you buy a bond, you are actually loaning your money to a company, like (General Electric) or a city, state or the federal government. For example, the City of Phoenix may want to expand their light rail, build a hospital or other municipal improvement. So they issue a bond to sell to investors and pay interest to those investors at a stated percentage on the bond. For example, a city issued bond may be a 10-year bond. Every year for 10 years the City of Phoenix pays you interest on the bonds you bought. If you bought a municipal bond for $100,000. You gave the city $100,000 of your money. The city pays you 6% or $6,000 interest every year. At the end of 10 years your interest received would amount to $60,000. Also at the end of 10 years the city would repay you your initial investment of $100,000. At the end of 10 years, your initial investment of $100,000 will have had a return of $160,000.

Bonds tend to be a desirable investment if you are looking for INCOME, as they have a set amount of interest that you are paid on a monthly or annual basis. Bond value, however, can fluctuate as interest rates on other bonds change. As long as you don't sell the bond or the bond is not called back by the issuer, you will continue to receive the interest regularly. One of the risks with bonds is that they can be "called" back by the issuer, which means that they pay you back your initial investment before the 10 years. While you will get paid your original investment, you now have $100,000 that you need to reinvest and you no longer have that $6,000 per year of interest income.

Stocks are another type of investment. Stocks are issued by companies to raise money in order to grow their business or to undertake new projects. You may have heard that buying stocks means you buy part ownership of a company or corporation. When you purchase stock in a company, what you actually buy is a share of the capital the company uses to operate. You are giving the company money to continue to operate, and you "share" in the company's profits. That is why stocks are also called "shares" and why you, as a stockholder, are also a "shareholder."

Some companies periodically will pay out profits to their shareholders in the form of a dividend. Before you buy a company's stock, you may want to know if that company pays out dividends so that you can match it with your goals of GROWTH OR INCOME.

If you want periodic payment returns on your stock, you should buy stock in a company that pays out dividends. Whether or not you want to receive periodic dividends, the value of your stock rises and falls with the profits of the company. You want to be certain you follow your trusted investment advisor's advice closely.

Investing with No Risk

It may seem crazy for me to say this but doing nothing may be a low-risk way of increasing your net worth. A savings account can be considered as an alternative method of "investing." By simply saving more and spending less you will increase your net worth. While there is a "cost" to keeping your money in cash, if you have zero risk tolerance (never want to see the value of your investments go down)then just hang on to the cash for a while. This may be a good short-term strategy while you build your wealth and have many unknown situations. You can have your money available. This is called 'LIQUIDITY". If your money is invested in stocks or bonds, it may take a few days to pull money out of your account for an emergency. However, if some of your investments are LIQUID, then you can access that money quickly. The only drawback to having all your money in cash is that in the long term, that money will have less value. For example, if you have $10,000 in cash, that will buy $10,000 of "stuff" today. However, in 10 years that "stuff" may cost $12,000. That's why you could have purchased Cadillac Eldorado 2 Door Convertible in 1954 for $5,738.

Having less buying power in the future is called INFLATION. Things cost more in the future, they always have and that always seems to continue. In general, savings accounts are not designed to generate more money through interest or dividends like bonds and stocks but are LOW RISK. If you put $100,000 in the bank, and leave it alone you will still have $100,000 next year. Savings accounts, because they are LIQUID, can be used to put money away for future use for perhaps a down payment on a house, tuition for college, or "for a rainy day". The money you put in a savings account stays there until you withdraw it.

There are several types of savings vehicles available, including: traditional savings accounts and certificate of deposit. Choosing the right one involves just a few steps.

1. Determine what you will be saving the money for.
2. Decide how much access you want to your money. Is it "liquid?"
3. Identify how much money you have to deposit.
4. Find the account with the best interest rate and lowest fees.

High liquidity means your money is available for you immediately. For example, if you want to be able to withdraw money at a moment's notice, you need an account that's very liquid.

Typically, a traditional savings account or checking account offers the highest liquidity. If you can leave your deposit amount untouched for a longer amount of time, you may want to consider a CD, or certificate of deposit. The longer you agree to leave your money, the better the interest rate. However, if you have to withdraw money before the agreed time is up, you will likely pay a significant penalty fee for doing so. Want to DOUBLE YOUR MONEY? See the Rule of 72 at the end of this book.

Another avenue to invest your wealth is to own a business. Your goal for owning a business may be growth (i.e. increase the value of a business and sell it), or income (i.e. create a business that produces income for you on a monthly basis).

The most important takeaway from this is that you must have an investment advisor and CPA that you trust, can freely direct questions toward, and can learn from. It's critical that you understand what your advisors are recommending you do with YOUR money.

Risks and Insurance

The other RISKS that do not involve investments were briefly mentioned above, but to offer you a bit more information, you can purchase, as we mentioned above, insurance to protect certain risks

Health Insurance – risk of injury or sickness to pay doctors and hospital bills

Life Insurance – risk of death to provide for your family/survivors

Long Term Care Insurance – as we get older in our society it is more likely that we will need help paying for living in an elder care facility. These current costs are as much as $10,000 per month in some cases.

Disability income insurance – you can protect against a loss of income if you were injured and unable to perform your job. Simple policies for doctors, lawyer and accountants are affordable and commonplace in business. Additionally, there are disability policies for athletes specific for Career Ending Injury (we have seen recent articles about collegiate athletes protecting their draft potential in their last year of school.) In addition, there are custom policies that can be developed for specific situations. This is common in the entertainment industry, for example a former client and jazz musician had his fingers insured by Lloyds of London.

Property Casualty Insurance – Your basic Home and Car Insurance is often overlooked, so make sure you have the right AMOUNT of coverage and a possible umbrella policy. If you become a high-profile individual it is important that you don't shop ONLY for the price, but also ensure that you have the right amount of coverage.

Takeaways, Questions and Actions:

1. How much of my money can I afford to lose?
2. What is your time horizon for investments?
3. How much do I have saved up and how long will that last me?
4. What is my biggest financial fear (i.e. what can't I risk)?

CHAPTER 6: CHOOSING THE TEAM

FINDING YOUR 'NO" PERSON

"No one's going to tell you "NO'
because they want to stay in your … circle"
(Eugene Profit, former NFL Player, Forbes.com)

The first thing I tell potential professional athlete clients is that I am your "NO" person. I tell them that if they don't want to say "no" to someone, have them call me and I will say "NO" for you. Also, I am straight with my clients. If I don't like an idea, a decision, an option or suggestion I will say "no." Many advisors, as Profit says in the Forbes.com article quoted above, are scared to say "no." As an athlete I ask that you respect when your advisor says "no." You do have a right to know why, but understand that their advice reflects years of professional experience and education. Listen to them, then you can make an informed and intelligent decision. I tell advisors who want to work with athletes two things: 1) don't be afraid to say "no" and 2) remember that it's their money and our job is to help them manage it.

Great advisors can be compared to "life coaches" because they can help you manage some of the complex financial decisions throughout your life such as buying a car, house, or saving for college. We deal with these decisions on a daily basis. In my career, I have negotiated the purchase of Ferraris, Bentleys, Range Rovers, McClarens, Porsches, Aston Martins as well as Fords, Jeeps and Chevys. Great advisors will help you reach your lifelong financial and personal goals.

When you are in the process of choosing your professional advisory team, it is important that you evaluate that team according to the advice and support they will give you when you are done playing. Most of the time, the remaining advisors are your investment advisor, your attorney (for estate planning and business), and your CPA. These are the ones who will help you transition to the next part of your life.

Working with your investment team both while you are playing and after you retire is important. Part of "working" with your team means understanding what they do, what recommendations they are making and more importantly WHY they are making those recommendations. Many young athletes that have received a large amount of money from a signing bonus or large salaries have said to me that they feel "dumb" asking questions. There is a misconception that RICH PEOPLE ARE SMART. While many wealthy individuals are smart, most of them have accumulated that education over years of working with professionals, trial and error as well as additional schooling. At 22 years old there is not an expectation that you should know everything just because you have money. Be aware that it is okay indeed to ask questions. IT IS YOUR MONEY and do not forget that.

Ask those Questions

Above all, don't be afraid to ask a question because you fear it may make you look dumb. I am a CPA and specialize in taxes. I have clients who are highly educated doctors who perform major operations such as heart transplants or brain surgery. Yet they know nothing about taxes and business. Taxes are not their specialty. If they ask a question about their taxes, it doesn't mean they're dumb. It only means they have not been educated in that field. Taxes are not your specialty. Your athletic abilities are. If you ask questions about your finances or taxes, it doesn't mean you're dumb. Always ask. Always keep informed.

The most important thing in choosing an advisor is to find someone with whom you can connect and build trust. By having more than one advisor you will have "another set of eyes" looking at your accounts.

Regarding that "three-legged stool of advisors" was mentioned in Chapter One, it's time to cover a little more about attorneys and their specialties. Be aware you may need more than one lawyer because you may need legal advice and representation for various things. For instance, for creating wills and passing along your assets to your heirs, you would need an estate planning attorney. If you have bought a franchise or have started your own business, you may need a business attorney to help with possible business problems or help you set up a corporation. Maybe a legal issue with your taxes might arise in which your CPA could not help. Then you would need a tax attorney. Maybe you want to sue someone, or perhaps you're being sued. You would need a litigating attorney or a defense attorney for those situations. You can use different lawyers for different purposes, depending upon what your legal needs are.

For your financial bookkeeping and tax preparation, a Certified Public Accountant is your best resource. Although regulations are a little different in each state, Certified Public Accountants must have over one-hundred and fifty hours of college-level accounting classes, must pass a six-part test (which can take 2 ½ days) as well as maintaining their licenses with forty hours of continuing education every year. CPAs are constantly improving their skills and being educated on changing tax laws. Many CPA's, like my firm, also offer business management services. Our firm not only deals with taxes, we also provide services and advice regarding business financing, business structure, large asset purchases like homes and autos, personal financial management, and other day-to-day financial needs. I mentioned earlier that you, as a professional athlete, operate like a small business; thus, the CPA acts as your CFO (Chief Financial Officer) managing your day-to-day business affairs as they are integrated into your long term and more advanced financial affairs.

An investment advisor is also part of your "three-pronged professional team." I mentioned that in Chapter One, but I would like to speak more about financial advisors because they are part of your continuing support group after you finish playing. Just like accountants become certified, so do financial advisors. Just as you want to have a Certified Public Accountant on your support team, you also want to have a Certified Financial Planner (CFP). CFPs have licenses to sell or invest stocks, bonds, or insurance. There are different types of licenses for financial planners, and becoming certified is not easy.

It takes two years for a financial planner to become certified. Prerequisites for certification include a Bachelor's Degree and three years of experience as a financial planner. A Certified Financial Planner can hold several types of licenses.

- Securities License – This license allows the CFP to sell mutual funds, life insurance, and investment trusts.
  To hold this license, the CFP must be able to manage all aspects of accounts and purchasing.
- Securities Agent – This license allows the CFP to purchase or sell mutual funds, stocks, or bonds.
- Uniform Investment License – This license allows the CFP to be an investment advisor.
- General Securities Representative – This license allows the CFP to be qualified to advise and answer information concerning general securities such as stocks, bonds, and investments.

The above is a very broad and general overview of different licenses a CFP may have and training a CFP must undergo. There are additional licenses a financial planner can obtain, such as a Series 65, Series 6 or Series 7, all of which allow them to sell different types of investments. It is enough to say that a financial planner must undergo detailed testing before he or she can become certified. Just as a Certified Public Accountant is the highest in his or her field, so is a Certified Financial Planner the highest in the financial planning field.

I briefly mentioned in Chapter One that a financial advisor or financial planner protects and grows your financial assets. That person's job is to assist with your selection of investments to fit your goals as well as your risk tolerance levels. While you're actively playing and earning money, you may have a high risk tolerance because you have a steady income. After you are off your team and "retired," your risk tolerance may change. Depending upon where you are in your life, you may have different investment goals and financial plans. To be certain those goals and plans are met, you need a Certified Financial Planner to explain your investments and to manage them. It is the CFP's job to help you understand your investments and how they are performing on an ongoing basis. It is his or her job to help you invest as wisely as you can so your financial needs are always met.

The US Securities and Exchange Commission (the SEC) www.sec.gov has fantastic information on investing and choosing a broker. Some of their advice is as follows and is worth repeating.

First, THINK through your financial objectives. This is where we talked about having goals and a plan.

Before you hire anyone:

- Talk and Meet with several firms. As we mentioned earlier, Kareem Abdul-Jabar lost investments because he simply went with the recommendation of other teammates.
- Perform a FINRA Broker Check, as we discussed earlier, to verify history of any past disciplinary actions.
- Understand HOW they will get paid. Is it commissions? Is it a percentage of assets under their management? Are there any additional fees?
- Find out if they are a member of Securities Investor Protection Corporation (SIPC), which provides limited protection if the broker becomes insolvent.

When opening an account there are still more questions to ask, including:

- Who will control the decision making on your account? Does the broker have the ability to make trades with our without your consent?
- Is there a provision to go "on margin" or borrow against your current investments for new investments? Going "on margin" means you are borrowing money to buy investments, which can be dangerous and has caused many wealthy investors to lose everything when the market declines.
- Never invest in a product you do not FULLY understand, and if you don't, get a second opinion from a CPA or another advisor.

Be Alert for:

- Recommendations based on "inside or confidential information", it's called INSIDER TRADING and it means GOING TO JAIL.
- Suspicious representations of spectacular profits, such as your money will "double in six months."
- Guarantees that you will NOT lose money or agreements that the broker will share in losses on your account.
- Watch for too many transactions in your account (also knows as "churning".)
- Any assurance that any error in your account is because of "computer or clerical error."

Always Looking Forward

There will come a time when the athlete part of your life is over. One of the challenges for any former athlete is the loss of your support. While you were playing you had coaches, teammates, your agent as well as perhaps a public relations firm, and the administration of the team or college. Suddenly, that support disappears. It will happen and it will happen quickly. As you are no longer part of a "team" you will have feelings of being alone with nowhere to go.

NOW, while you are still in the game, is the time to begin looking ahead to your transition from being an active-athlete to being a former-athlete. As you prepare for your future of "civilian life," it is important to understand that you will continue to need a professional support team, your "three-professional team," that you now have. Your current support team may not be the same one that you will need moving to your post-athletic career. You may need different areas of expertise to support you as you transition. Your transition does not have to be one of anxiety or dread. It can and should be one of excitement and anticipation as you move to remake yourself bolstered by a solid support team.

Follow up to Choosing your Advisor: Separation of Duties

As a CPA we are taught to develop internal controls in a business to minimize the likelihood of fraud. One of those first aspects of internal control is the separation of duties. That means that no single person does everything. For instance, the person that collects the money does not reconcile the bank statements. By instituting separation of duties in any business, you minimize the likelihood of fraud. While you can never completely eliminate fraud, it is a risk you can minimize.

When a player comes to me and says "oh my agent handles everything" or "my financial advisor handles everything" I always stop and take a breath and try to explain the dangers of such arrangements.

While having one person or one company handling every aspect of your personal and business life does not necessarily mean that you will be defrauded, or that you will lose money; it increases the likelihood of that happening. That is why I always explain the importance of having those three professionals operating as separate advisors, while still working together.

You must remember that as an athlete people will always tell you "you're the quarterback" in the NFL or that "you're the manager" in baseball or they will remind you that "you're the captain of the team". However you are actually the OWNER of the entire team. It is all your money, and that's very important for you to remember. You are the one that hires and fires the coach, hires and fires the manager, hires and fires the offensive coordinator, hires and fires the pitching coach, or the batting coach. Everybody works FOR you.

I do not want to scare anyone into thinking that just because one person is doing everything that fraud will occur. While there are some fantastic organizations that have such broad knowledge that they actually can do everything and do it well, many others promise that service, but fail miserably. The main problem is that you are most likely not educated enough in taxes, law and investments to know if they are taking the correct action or not.

It's critical to ensure that your three advisors, your agent/attorney, your investment advisor, and your CPA are working together. While they should be collaborating for your best interest, they will also watch out for you individually to make sure that you are getting the best advice.

Many times I will call an agent and say "hey, we have an issue with our client", or I will call the investment advisor to work on end of year tax planning ideas. In my experience the most overlooked member of your team is the CPA, not because I am a CPA, but because as a CPA I bring a different level of knowledge that an agent or investment advisor may not possess.

I had an investment advisor tell me that they did not want to take any deductions because they were afraid of the IRS. What that indicates to me is that the advisor did not understand tax law. Their firm has either had a bad experience or absolutely no experience with an IRS audit and a capable CPA. There are two things that we say in our profession. First, "Pigs get fat, hogs get slaughtered, don't be a hog".

In addition, famous Judge Learned Hand once stated regarding income taxes, "Anyone may arrange his affairs so that his taxes shall be as low as possible; he is not bound to choose that pattern which best pays the treasury. There is not even a patriotic duty to increase one's taxes or public duty to pay more than the law demands." -Judge Learned Hand, Helvering v. Gregory, 69 F.2d 809, 810 (2d Cir. 1934), aff'd, 293 U.S. 465 (1935)

When you start picking your team, make sure you pick a team that you think will work together and be able to act independently from one another. Make sure that if you want to terminate one of the three, that it won't affect your relationship with the other two. Make sure that if one of the three is not acting in your best interest, the other two will let you know. It is unfortunate that you have to create this system of checks and balances, but not having the knowledge of the law, investments or taxation, you cannot possibly know if the answers you are getting are in your best interest.

Takeaways, Questions and Actions:

1. Find at least one CPA – Talk to him/her.
2. Find at least one Attorney – Talk to him/her.
3. Find at least one Investment Advisor – Talk to him/her.

CHAPTER 7: TRANSITION

Of the NCAA student athletes,
Percentages that go pro in the US (NCAA, 2017)

Baseball 9.1%
Men's Basketball 1.1%
Women's Basketball .09%
Hockey 5.6%
Soccer 1.6%
Football 1.5%

I don't quote the above to discourage you but to make sure that, no matter what, you plan during your collegiate career for the moment when you become and ex-athlete.

Previously, I mentioned your transition from athlete to civilian life. The dictionary defines transition as "a process or period in which something undergoes a change and passes from one state, stage, form, or activity to another." You will eventually undergo a change from being an athlete to a second career.

Transition – change – can sometimes be difficult for anybody who's been doing the same thing for a number of years. What we do for much of our lives can define us and who we are. You meet someone at a party, and you say, "Glad to meet you. What do you do?" "Oh," they may reply, "I'm a Doctor." Or "I'm a Police officer." Or "I'm a teacher." We closely identify ourselves with our professions. Our professions become part of us, and when we undergo a change from our professions, many times it feels as if our inner selves change also. Irrationally, we may feel like a shell of our former selves.

If transition comes abruptly through an injury, being released from a team, or not being signed as a free agent, the process is no different than being fired from any job. Getting fired happens quickly and no matter how well prepared you are, (or even how much you say "I hate this job, I wish they would fire me,)" it can be a stunner. As a collegiate athlete, you may know that your athletic career is coming to a close, or you may hope that you get drafted, only to be left undrafted. If you are lucky enough to become a professional athlete, your career will still end at one point and you must have a plan in place when that ending comes. You want to have your backup plan ready to go when your change happens, whether that change is abrupt and unexpected or whether you play to the end of a long career.

This is a good time for a reminder of what Taylor Pak said in her book *Fit for Business*,

> "It's fair to say that the recruiting process is equitable to the job search, which means that student athletes already have a great deal of practice. Finding the right home for your unique personality and skill set is not an easy task. It takes research (again lots of research) and some time to figure out what your strengths and weaknesses are."

Transitioning from athlete to civilian life takes an average of three years for most athletes. Whether collegiate or professional, this is all you have done since you were a young child. For professional athletes, those three years is when most financial problems occur. ESPN and Sports Illustrated provided statistics that 78% of former professional athletes run into financial issues during those first three years. Usually those problems and issues arise because the athlete did not have a financial plan already in place before his or her transition happened. Even if you have a plan in place, adjusting to your new civilian life can be difficult. Suddenly your schedule is not what it had been for years. Suddenly your life is no longer scheduled for you. You are now 100% in control of your life and that's not something most athletes are used to.

I have spoken to many former professional athletes regarding their transition experience, and I find a common thread for all athletes. (this is very similar to Military to Civilian life)

1. Year ONE - Most have discussed how the first year is taken up by merely adjusting to the fact they are no longer on a team, for some it was still training to get "back in the game" or waiting for the call that did not come.
2. Year TWO is spent in evaluating their options, finishing school if they did not have their degree and investigating potential jobs.
3. Year THREE is spent executing the plan.

This chapter is about the transition. Your goal is to understand how to psychologically prepare yourself for when your athletic career ends before it ends. That can be a tough challenge for any collegiate or professional athlete because you are expected to train to be the best athlete possible. It's a challenge to think about life after sport because you have to concentrate on practice every day (and school if you are a college athlete) and prepare for game day. Somehow you must learn to balance your concentration on your present career with your consideration of your future one.

My interviews have a common response. There WILL come a time when there is no one telling you to get up, where to be, when to be where, when practice is, when dinner is, when and where the meeting is, and telling you it's lights out, "bed check." Basically, someone else has scheduled your life as an athlete for ten, fifteen, or more years. The point most former athletes make is that if you think it's hard being on a schedule, it's harder not to be. Adjusting to life without restrictions can be as hard as adjusting to strict ones, and you must be mentally prepared to understand your life will be very different when your athletic career ends.

As a highly performing athlete, you probably have been "playing your game" for a long time, perhaps since you were eight or ten years old. As a child, adults "scheduled" your life at home and at school. In college you had to follow a schedule of classes and your team's schedule. As a professional athlete, you also are following your coach's and your team's rigid schedule. When your athletic career is over, there is no one to schedule your life but yourself. You are free. You don't have to maintain a schedule if you don't want to. You can stay out all night and sleep all day. Many times this is when depression will hit former athletes. To follow a schedule means you are more in control of your life than if you do not follow a schedule.

Unless you have a transition plan in place for your life, when you come to the end of your athletic career, you come to your "What do I do now?" moment. If you are in your 20's or 30's, your "What do I do now?" question is a question of "What do I do for the next 40 or 50 years?"

It is for this reason that you should start building the tools necessary to survive post career NOW. Start using the tools and advantages you have as an athlete to do what we talked about in the other chapters. Build your brand. Network. Investigate and ask questions. You may not find the answer now, but you will have a good head start.

What profession would you like to be in? Once you decide, start moving in the direction of where you want to go. For example, if you would like to be in broadcasting, begin making acquaintances, network, take workshops, or intern with a network. This goes back to networking. Network with as many people as you can in whatever profession you are interested for when your athletic career is done.

A good "tool" to have in preparing yourself for your transition is a personal mission statement. Whatever it is you want to do after your athletic career, whatever it is you want to be, it is good to know and understand what your personal mission is. It is good to begin working with your mission statement as soon as you can before the end of your athletic career. Start planning now. Set your goals. That's what a mission statement is. It's setting and defining your goals you want to attain.

What type of industries interest you? Research and use your network of people to find resources in those industries. Perhaps in the off season volunteer as an intern to do work in something that interests you. Volunteering is a great foot-in-the-door strategy.

What is it that you want to accomplish? What is it you want to leave behind as your legacy? What are your core values? Your personal mission statement helps guide you in the direction you want to go. It helps you to think more deeply about your life, clarify your purpose, and identify what is truly important to you.

Why do you need a personal mission statement? To determine the direction in which you want to go. Writing a mission statement is an act of self-discovery. Some examples of personal mission statements are:

- Oprah Winfrey – "To be a teacher. And to be known for inspiring my students to be more than they thought they could be."
- Richard Branson, multi-millionaire founder of The Virgin Group – "To have fun in my journey through life and learn from my mistakes."
- Denise Morrison, CEO of Campbell Soup Company – "To serve as a leader, live a balanced life, and apply ethical principles to make a significant difference."
- Microsoft – "Our mission is to empower every person and every organization on the planet to achieve more."
- Google – "To organize the world's information and make it universally accessible and useful."

Five questions to ask yourself in crafting your personal mission statement are:

- What is important and valuable to me?
- Where do I want to go in my life?

- What does "the best" look like to me?
- How do I want people to describe me?
- What kind of legacy do I want to leave behind?

Keep your statement short. Remember your statement is just as much about the people you want to impact as it is about yourself. Share your statement with trusted friends and family who might provide you with valuable insights about yourself and your statement. Don't be afraid to make changes, because as you grow and evolve, your mission may also. As a successful professional athlete, you have an opportunity to give back to your community. Perhaps that idea could be part of your mission statement also.

When you consider what your mission statement will be, there is an acronym or abbreviation that may help you. It is S.M.A.R.T. You want a "smart" statement. Those letters stand for:

S – Specific. Be specific in stating your goals.
M – Measurable. Set limits to your goals. Make them something you can do.
A – Achievable. Make your goals something you can achieve.
R – Relevant. Make your goals logical to you.
T – Time Bound. Set a target date to reach your goal.
Making your goals "Time Bound" sets a timeline to prevent procrastination.

Finally, what skills do you have that can help you in your transition to your new life? What is your personality? How have you gotten along with your teammates, front office staff, and coaches?

How do you handle wins and losses? Possibly one of the best skills you can develop while a professional athlete is the skill of handling adversity.

In her book *Fit for Business,* Taylor Pak discusses that during most of your collegiate athletic career you have been gaining all the necessary experiences to develop a skillset that is perfect for the business world. "Athletes are capable professionals that all have the key qualities to succeed in life. By the time their collegiate sports careers are over, athletes will have spent countless hours training and investing their time in a sport that, up until this point, has very much defined their existence." She goes on to say that her entire life had been about her identity as an athlete. She states that what she "learned during the game" prepared her for life "after the game".

Taylor and Ogilvie (1984) in the Journal of Applied Sports Psychology, introduced the conceptual model of transition. The Society for Sport, Exercise and Performance Psychology newsletter issue from May 2016 talks about TRANSFERRABLE SKILLS that include the ability to perform under pressure, problem solving, organizational skills, ability to meet deadlines and challenges, setting and achieving goals, dedication, self-motivation and team related interpersonal skills.

Floyd Little, NFL Hall of Famer, says that all collegiate athletes have the keys to success, and they are Drive, Determination, Dedication, Desire, Commitment and Sacrifice.

For example, losing a big game by one point and having to go back the coming weekend and play again before the home crowd is really no different than working really hard to make a sale and losing it or spending hours developing a wonderful marketing presentation and losing the client you were trying to win. They are both losses involving adversity or unfavorable and unpleasant experiences.

A player who was been traded during his career to more than just a few teams told me that the experience allowed him to be able to integrate into any team. It was, he said, no different than stepping into a new job in a new office and learning to work with new co-workers. Additionally, with new coaches and new teams came a new "system" that he had to learn. While in the business world, his skill and ability to learn an entirely new playbook meant he feel comfortable learning a new company's business methods.

Another great transitional skill you have learned as a professional athlete is striving for a goal. As a team member, you wanted your team to win. Therefore, you have the skill of being competitive. You want yourself and your business team to achieve the goals you have set for yourself and the ones your business team has set for itself.

Most of all, as an athlete, you want to continually improve your skills and your game. "Better today than yesterday." You can transfer that skill, that mindset, into the business world as you transition from your old life to your new one.

Takeaways, Questions and Actions:

1. If I was NOT an athlete, what would I want to be?
2. What are the necessary steps to achieve that goal?
3. List 5 things that you have learned during your athletic career.
4. List 3 events that you experienced that make you a great employee.

CHAPTER 8: WHAT DO I DO NOW?

The question is "What do I do now?" I could ask it a bit differently, "What do YOU do now?" You've read through the book, and, hopefully, you've learned how to find a good advisor and support team. Maybe you've learned something about how banks work and how to protect your credit. Perhaps you've learned something about networking and investments. If you haven't considered your mission statement yet, this is a good time to do it. After you finish reading this chapter, this would also be a good time to find your trusted advisor/ mentor if you haven't found that person yet. Maybe the person is a family member. Maybe he or she is a good friend. Take this book with you to that person. Go through it with your advisor. Discuss the questions and your answers.

In other words, you have read the book. You may have thought about your mission statement. Now take action! Is there a certain industry that interests you, a position you might like after your athletic career is over? Set up a meeting with someone in that industry. You want to do this before your athletic career is over because you have more leverage as a collegiate or professional athlete still "in the game". Use that leverage to arrange a meeting with a local business owner or professional in the industry of your interest. Such an opportunity is available to almost any athlete at any time in any city. Remember your brand? Remember how to build and extend the life of your brand? Remember the "time" and "distance" of your brand? Use your brand while it still has its "time" and "distance."

To recap and summarize, I want to re-emphasize your "three professional team." As I said at the beginning of this book, everyone will need a supportive "team." The three professionals approach is critical for maintaining and sustaining solid foundations to support a post athletic career lifestyle. Those three "professional legs" are an attorney, an investment advisor, and a Certified Public Accountant. You want a balanced and objective support team. You need this support system, and, if you don't presently have it, you want to start building it now. If you don't understand the importance of your support system, please re-read the chapter over again until you do. Your "three-professional support system" is essential to your success as an active or former collegiate or professional athlete and as you transition to civilian life.

As an active professional athlete, you will not have as much time as you think to manage your affairs like so-called "normal people" or civilians do. That's why you need your "three-legged" support system to help with different aspects of your life. You need an attorney to help you understand and navigate legal matters, estate planning, intellectual property rights, copyrights and protection of your name and likeness. Your agent, as an attorney, will be critical during your career for such legal matters as contracts, but you also need someone well-versed in family, business and perhaps franchise law. You need a financial advisor or investment counselor to help you with your investment choices that will protect and grow your savings in accordance with your goals, both short term and long term. Finally, with the complex and always changing tax laws, you will need a CPA to help you manage your personal day to day finances as well as to integrate your personal and business tax structure.

If you are lucky enough to play professionally in the sport you love, you will become a small company. Your personal life will end up being handled like a small business. A business manager can help with the management of expenses, monitoring day to day spending, ensuring that you keep on track with your budget. Along with the other professionals, your CPA, attorney, and investment advisor, you will create the management team necessary to survive life as a professional athlete. People will tell you that you are the quarterback or the coach, but you should consider yourself as the OWNER of the team. It's your money and everyone works FOR you. Don't forget it.

So now take action. If you don't have a trusted advisor or even a mentor, start looking for someone to fit that role. Because I have dealt with the "what do I do now" question for the past 30 years, I am happy to help any young athlete navigate the transition from collegiate to professional sports, from professional sports to "civilian" life or from collegiate athletics to post college reality.

I'm always willing to help steer you in a direction, work out what your short and long term goals might be, or provide you with suggestions of how to start.

You will come to your "What do I do now?" moment. Perhaps you already have. How do you answer the question? As I have emphasized throughout this book, preparation is the key to your answer. The dictionary defines preparation as "something done in advance in order to be ready for a future event." So prepare! Begin now! Take action! You have already taken your first step by reading this book. Take your next step. Find your trusted advisor. Build your support team. Lay your groundwork and build upon it. Continue taking your steps. And walk into your bright, stable, and rewarding future.

Takeaways, Questions and Actions:

- Look at your resources, both financial and personal.
- Understand your income and expenses.
- Set goals (Where do you see yourself in 5-10-15 years).
- Identify and evaluate the steps on how to accomplish them.
- Put the steps to reach your goals into action.
- Review your progress with your team.
- Make adjustments if needed and get help if it's not working.

CHAPTER 9: TAXES AND BUSINESS

I would be remiss if I did not give you a few tax tips. As a CPA/ business manager, it is my job to ensure that you are compliant with all of the tax regulations and to ensure that you take advantage of any deductions you are entitled to take under the law. Additionally, it is my job to act as your CFO for you and your businesses.

The primary place to start is when you get paid and how you get paid. If you are on a team sport, you are an employee. IRS rules dictate how you get paid. In the late 70's early 80's Gary Sargent, a Minnesota North Star player tried to argue that he should be paid not as an employee but as an independent contractor, allowing him to deduct his expenses of being a professional hockey player. The IRS ruled against him, and now all team players are employees and receive a W2. If you play an individual sport, like golf, tennis or swimming, then you can have your income directed to a "loan out corporation" and take advantage of business expenses deducted from your income.

However, be aware that the employee payroll process automatically takes the mandatory taxes from your paycheck and as long as you have correct withholdings calculated, therefore you may be safe with taxes. If, however, you are a solo athlete, then you must determine your budget for necessary taxes. If so, how much do you have to save in your budget for taxes? Everyone's situation is different. That is why you must have your team of professionals working with your budget.

Taxes as an EMPLOYEE

Federal Income Taxes are based on your overall worldwide earnings. It means your wages, interest, dividends, and gains from the sale of stocks as well as royalties, appearance income, or endorsement income. The federal tax law is complicated and the changes in 2018 alone created a whole host of new issues that will require the services of a CPA to make sure you are in compliance. The dangers of not paying your federal taxes range from being charged penalties and interest for not paying on time, to taking money out of your bank or putting a lien against your home, to JAIL. Yes, jail. Westley Snipes recently went to jail because he was advised that he did not need to pay income taxes. Needless to say, that was not wise advice. Federal taxes range from 10% to 37% of your income.

FICA and Medicare (Social Security taxes) are taken out of your paycheck and can amount to tens of thousands of dollars if you are a high wage earner. If you have a regular job, it can be close to 8% of your income taken out of your salary.

State taxes can be a little as zero if you live in Texas, but as much as 13-14% in other states.

While the tax rates are variable, if you add them together, it can be as much as 50% of your income going to taxes. Remember that $1,000,000 bonus check? You can expect to get $500,000 after taxes, and that's where you start to budget your money wisely.

TAXES AS A BUSINESS

If you are in an individual sport, be smart enough to create what's commonly referred to as "a loan-out" corporation, or perhaps start your own business. This makes your financial world a whole lot more complicated than we can discuss in this book. Needless to say, it requires the services of a CPA/Business manager to do just that, "manage the business."

DEDUCTIONS

Until 2018 you were able to deduct expenses related to your job. As a professional athlete that meant your agent commissions. In 2018 that changed and you are no longer allowed to take those deductions. What is a DEDUCTION? In simple terms, it is an expense that you spend related to your job, and this will reduce your TAXABLE INCOME by the amount you spent. While the law no longer allows this for 2018, in simple terms, if you earn $100,000 in endorsement money, but spent $12,500 to earn that money for travel or supplies, you would only pay tax on 100,000 – 12,500 = 87,500. In taxes, you would save the expense ($12,500) times the tax rate (example 30%). By taking the allowed deduction you would have saved $3,750 in cold hard cash. What can I Deduct? I get that question a lot. The answer depends on many factors, but here is a list of some of the items that an athlete can deduct: auto expenses, airfare, hotel, meals, training costs, athletic equipment, legal fees, accounting fees, internet, computer, telephone, marketing costs, public relations, advertising, etc. For each of those you will need to keep information on the who, what, where, when, and why of each expenses. Complicated? Confusing? You bet. But that's what a CPA/ business manager is for.

I WANT TO BE AN ENTREPRENEUR

Entrepreneurship is the process of starting your own business. It is closely aligned with franchises as I will discuss in more detail. However, unlike buying a franchise from an already-existing business, an entrepreneur generally starts a business from nothing. A simple definition of an entrepreneur is someone with the ability, resources, and willingness to develop, organize, and manage a business venture along with any of its risks, in order to make a profit. An entrepreneur usually risks his or her own money to begin a business.

Being an entrepreneur takes solid self-belief that you can start and develop your business idea. It takes hard work and disciplined dedication. Entrepreneurs believe in themselves, are confident and dedicated to their project. They are willing to work hard and face long odds of being successful. They are creative thinkers, risk takers, and have strong work ethics. In my experience, and in my opinion, a person just can't "become" an entrepreneur. If you are interested in owning your own business, you can learn from others. If you want to "be an entrepreneur," the best thing to do is to find someone who is in the field you're interested in and learn from that person. Entrepreneurship is more than just wanting to be a business owner. Some people are cut out to be business owners and some, unfortunately, are not. Always go to your support team of professionals to discuss what you want to do and look to your professionals and their resources to make sure you make a well informed and smart decision.

A popular way to start a business is to purchase a franchise. While still very risky, a franchise allows you to buy a successful business' trademark, concept and "know how" and then sell its products or services. For example, McDonald's, Pizza Hut, 7-Eleven, or UPS Store. A franchise is a "business in a box."

When you buy a franchise, you buy all the instructions of how to build, open, run, and manage whatever business it is, whether it is a McDonald's, a hotel, or a gym. You pay an upfront fee to buy the franchise rights, and then you pay regular royalty fees for the use of those rights. Upfront fees vary widely, some are more affordable than others.

Having a franchise means you also have that company's national marketing and brand name supporting your business. If you decide to buy a McDonald's franchise, you automatically have bought a brand name and logo that is instantly recognized throughout the world. An easily recognizable and familiar brand is a good choice for your franchise if you decide to invest your money in one.

The reason this concept is popular with many athletes is because a franchise comes with a "game plan." When you buy a franchise, you also buy its "playbook" of instructions of how to "run their offense" (sales) and "develop their defense" (cost management) or "building their teams" (staff and employee management). Your franchisor, in effect, is your coach. You are guided, instructed, and coached on how the franchise works and how you need to run it to be successful when you don't know anything about the business.

As with any business, there are risks purchasing and operating a franchise. You may follow all the rules and your franchise may still not be successful. It could be your location. Maybe what works in California doesn't work in Texas. With a franchise, you can minimize the risk of starting a business from scratch, by having the support and know-how of the franchisor, its marketing, and its company team to help you and back you up.

How do you pick a franchise? You need to look at all the same variables of any business. Is it retail? Is it going to be open 24 hours? Is it open weekends? Is it a service business? Do you have to manage inventory?

In evaluating a franchise, the most important aspect will be something that interests you. Secondly, if possible, you should pick a business in which you have some knowledge, more importantly, that you know someone who is an expert in the industry. You should carefully research all aspects of the franchise you're considering to buy and be certain it is right for you. You most certainly need to always keep your attorney, investment advisor, and CPA closely informed and continuously seek their input.

Alternatively, you could also be a "silent partner" as a franchisee. Maybe you know a trusted friend who has years of experience in a certain industry and wants to partner with you to open a franchise. While you are considered a "silent partner," that does not mean you "set it and forget it." It just means that the business does not need you to be involved in the day-to-day operations.

If you do consider buying a franchise or any business, it is absolutely necessary that you consult all of the professionals on your team. Your financial advisory team can help evaluate the amount you can afford to risk and invest. The team would review a pro forma and projections to analyze the financial health of the business you want to buy. You will use your attorney to review the legal documents involved. The main document in a franchise is called the FDD or "franchise development document," a 300-400 page document with rules, disclosures and spells out EXACTLY what the franchisor WILL and NOT do. There are, in fact, attorneys that specialize in the franchise industry. I strongly suggest that you seek the help of a specialized franchise attorney.

Regardless of your investment decisions, the risk involved, your choices of stock, bonds or just saving money, you always want to consult with your professional financial advisor. Investing is for your future, and you want to be sure to the best of your knowledge and your advisors' knowledge that your investments will provide a stable and comfortable financial future for you.

CHECKLIST FOR STARTING A BUSINESS

Many times new clients come to meet with me after they have already started a business, while some come before they start to be sure they do it correctly. If not done correctly, you will have to pay for fixing your errors and getting you on track. Here are the basics of starting your own business:

- Create a Business Plan – seek a CPA to help you create your plan, just like a game plan for the business.
- Formation – What type of company are you going to be? A C-Corporation, an S-Corporation, a Partnership, and LLC,

PLLC, LLLP. Each of these types of entities should be carefully chosen BEFORE you get started.

- State License and Registration (Which state, Delaware? Wyoming?).
- Federal Tax Identification Number (its free from the IRS).
- Funding – Where will you get the money? Until you have the first two figured out, no one will loan you money. If you have the ability to use your own money, don't. The best way to fund a business may be O.P.M. (Other People's Money), which can be through loans or sales of stock/interest.
- Licenses, Permits, Taxes, and Insurance – do you need a state license? city license? permit? payroll taxes? sales tax? unemployment insurance? liability insurance?
- Setting up the operational structure - payroll, banking, accepting credit cards.
- Employees – if you are going to have employees you will need help with compliance with FEDERAL and STATE laws, withholding requirements, and additional human resources including benefits like health insurance, OSHA, HIPPA, ACA and many other letters.
- Marketing your new business.

Regardless of starting your own company or working as an employee, you MUST understand the complexity of the tax, employment, legal requirements are more than one person can handle without the advice of a CPA and an Attorney.

CONCLUSION

People ask me, "why do I care" about student athletes? "Why do I care" about professional athletes doing stupid stuff? "Why do I do what I do?" The reason we should all care about the financial wellbeing and financial success of professional athletes is because of their impact on our society.

Danny Schayes in his book *Fast Broke* states, "The system is rigged for you to fail; the system uses many tricks to keep you confused, poorly educated and dependent on others." His book further explores the issues with chapters such as: It's in no one's interest that you "get it" and How to go broke on 100 Million. Because of people like Danny, who feel that the system failed them and forced them to figure it out on their own, there is an inherent need to fix the system. The WHY is because of what successful athletes can do for their communities.

Professional and retired athletes have long term effects of their success on the community at large. I believe that successful athletes are able to give back more to their communities when they are not themselves a drain on society. Through financial support and volunteer work, athletes, in general, are one of the most philanthropic groups of professionals.

In her dissertation, The Value and Contributions of the Participation in Intercollegiate Athletics on the Personal Development of Community College-Aged Students, Michelle Gill states that there is an "importance for student participants to develop their self-identity and a need to belong to as an accepted member with student peers." Furthermore, that the bonding was a "valued outcome of the experience of participating in intercollegiate athletics."

The students revealed that there were a number of life skills/ softs skills that were also learned from their participation, including confidence, trust, setting and completing goals, and leadership skills, and that these skills made them "individually stronger and more mature."

I spent 7 years as a summer camp counselor with teenagers as my "students." The very wise director gave the senior staff some sage advice. He said, "you cannot change in one month what it has taken a parent 14 years to "screw" up." In the case of young athletes, unfortunately, society and social media have had such an impact on the views and actions of young men and women that it is rather difficult to take a young newly minted millionaire and try to change behavior. We had over 300 children come through the camp every summer and the director's second piece of sage advice was the following: "if you affect the life of ONE child this summer, you have done your job." While we may not be able to save the world, if each of us can educate and connect with one student each year, then we, as stewards of the knowledge, have done our job.

Furthermore, in looking at the affect that one young athlete has on the community can be seen in the philanthropic work of NCAA and Professional athletes, active and former. The NCAA shows that 56 percent of male and 67 percent of female student athletes believe they have a responsibility to participate in volunteer or service activities in their community and more than 80 percent volunteer at least once a year. (www.ncaa.org)

Additionally, the professional sports industry in North America has increasingly focused on social responsibility over the past 10 years, and sports philanthropy has emerged as a key element of these activities. (Sheth/Babiak 2010)

Sports executives are increasingly becoming concerned with the image and public perception of their teams and, as such, reaching out to the communities in which they operate (Armey,2004) According to www.Charitynavigator.com (2009) Andre Agassi has one of the largest athletes charitable foundations with assets in excess of 80 million dollars. While you don't need to have that much to have an impact, others, such as Ndamukong Sug was the 6th most generous celebrity with over 2 million to the Nebraska University's athletic department and another $600,000 to the University of Nebraska Lincoln College of Engineering, which is the largest single gift from a former football player. (Forbes,2012)

Others include NBA's Carmello Athony's foundation providing gifts over $800,000 to Syracuse's The Living Classroom Foundation. The Chris Paul Family Foundation convened this group initially based on their mutual passions and because of the alignment of their work to the TRHT goals and framework. In the past, Chris Paul, Carmelo Anthony, Dwyane Wade, and LeBron James have used their voices to promote positive social change. (looktothestars.org, 2019)

In 2014 James Brown, former center for the then St. Louis Rams left the NFL to pursue farming. His First Fruits Farm continues to donate all their crops and, to date, has provided over 850,000 pounds of sweet potatoes and cucumbers to those in need.

EACH of these players would NOT be able to perform these incredible acts of philanthropy if they somehow were subject to financial disaster, victims of fraud, or provided inappropriate guidance on how to manage their assets during their playing days.

Because of the profound effect that these athletes have on their communities is the reason that we should care about the financial success of all athletes.

My personal mission has been crafted after 30 years in the business of Sports and Entertainment both from the inside as an advisor and as an outside observer:

> To educate my clients, associates, friends, and family using my education, experience and knowledge. To simplify the complex, allowing them to be successful and reach their personal financial goals. To empower, through education, young athletes to be successful long term and contribute to their community. To leave a legacy of education and knowledge for future generations to be successful and self-sufficient and leave the world and my community better than when I received it. To take advantage of what I am provided and be thankful and aware of the world around me.

APPENDIX I LARGE ASSET PURCHASES - CARS AND HOMES

(source Visa Financial Soccer, 2012,2018)

I did not want to overload you with too much information, so I wanted to make sure you knew how complicated and how intricate the two largest purchases you may make in your life can be.

When shopping for a car

1. Decisions
   - Deciding how much to spend (Need vs Wants)
   - How to Pay for it All Cash or Car Loan
   - Do I get New or Used
   - How do I Finance it? Lease or Purchase

2. Private Party or Dealer or Carvana online
   - If you decide on a used car from a dealer
   - Consider costs, reliability, dealer reputation
   - Research Carfax, Edmunds, KBB etc.

3. Consider the warranty and the service contract
   - What to do if you have problems
   - A used car from a private party
   - Sometimes includes a manufacturer's warranty
   - Difference in price compared to a dealer

4. A new car
   - Read about new car features and prices
   - Shop around
   - Plan to negotiate price
   - Learn the terms
   - Consider the service contract

Car Loans

What to consider when shopping for a car loan

- Annual Percentage Rate of Interest
- Length of loan
- Monthly payments
- Total finance charge
- Total to be repaid
- Shop around for a car loan and compare the Interest Rate
- What is a Lease? How is it different from a Loan/ Purchase?
- What is a co-signer?
- Understand the circumstances under which a vehicle can be repossessed, and list the legal
- Rights and responsibilities of the creditor and of the debtor

The cost to own, operate, and maintain a car

- o Initial purchase price
- o Registration and title costs
- o Sales tax
- o Financing cost
- o Insurance
- o Scheduled maintenance
- o Unscheduled repairs and maintenance
- o Gasoline, oil and other fluids
- o Parking and tolls

About warranties and service contracts

1. Types of warranties
    - o As-is warranty
    - o Implied warranty
    - o Dealer warranty
    - o Manufacturer's warranty

2. Service contracts
3. Preventing problems
4. Resolving disputes
5. Comparing promises of warranties and service contract

About auto insurance

1. Importance of and legal requirements
2. Types of coverage
    - o Bodily injury liability
    - o Property damage liability

- Collision
- Comprehensive
- Medical payments
- Uninsured motorist
- Rental reimbursement
- Towing and labor

3. How insurance rates are set
    - Age
    - Sex
    - Marital status
    - Personal habits (e.g., smoking)
    - Type of use
    - Frequency of use
    - Location
    - Driving record deductible
    - Type of car
    - Value and age of car

BUYING A HOME

First, SHOULD I buy or Rent

Comparing renting and buying

1. Main advantages of renting are:
    - Ease of mobility – Lock it and Leave it
    - Fewer responsibilities
    - Lower initial costs – no cost for repairs and Maintenance

2. Common disadvantages of renting are:
    - Few financial benefits in the form of tax deductions

- Restricted lifestyle, decorating, having pets, and other activities
- Legal concerns (landlords and neighbors)
- No opportunity to have the value of a home

3. Key benefits of buying your housing are:
    - Tax savings
    - Pride of ownership
    - Potential economic gain

4. Disadvantages of buying your house may include:
    - Financial risks related to having down payment funds, obtaining a mortgage, fluctuating property values
    - Limited mobility if a home is difficult to sell
    - Higher living costs due to repairs and maintenance

BUYING A HOME, The process

1. Phase 1 - How much home do you NEED vs WANT
2. Phase 2 - Location Location Location
3. Phase 3 - Finding a home within your Price
4. Phase 4 - Finance and Close
    - Applying for a mortgage
        - Determine an estimated value of the house
        - Obtain funds for a down payment
        - Know your credit score
        - Compare fees, services, and mortgage rates for different lenders
    - Prepare the mortgage application
        - types of mortgages

    - A conventional mortgage has equal payments, typically over 15, 30, or 40 years based on a fixed interest rate
    - Government-guaranteed financing programs include loans from the Federal Housing Authority (FHA) and the Veterans Administration (VA)
    - A balloon mortgage has fixed monthly payments and a very large final payment, usually after three, five, or seven years
    - The adjustable rate mortgage (ARM), also referred to as a flexible rate mortgage or a variable rate mortgage, has an interest rate that increases or decreases during the life of the loan based on changes in market interest rates
    - A graduated payment mortgage has payments rising to different levels during the term of the loan
    - An interest-only mortgage consists of interest-only payments for a specified period, usually five to ten years
    - Reverse mortgages provide an elderly homeowner with tax-free income in the form of a loan that is paid back (with interest) when the home is sold or the homeowner dies
    - Refinancing refers to obtaining a new mortgage on your current home at a lower interest rate
  - Selecting a mortgage
    - Shop around for mortgages through multiple lenders

    - Estimate a mortgage payment based on different factors including interest rates and different terms of the loan closing costs

- The common costs associated with the settlement of a real estate transaction may include:
    - Attorney or escrow fees
    - Title insurance
    - Property taxes
    - Appraisal fee
    - Recording fees, transfer taxes
    - Loan discount points
    - Inspections
    - Lender's origination fee
    - Reserves for home insurance and property taxes
    - Interest (paid from date of closing to 30 days before first monthly payment)
    - Real estate agent commission

APPENDIX II MONEY AND CREDIT

Why Budget?

- Helps you to live within your means and meet expenses
- Helps you save for long- and short-term goals
- Giving you goals to achieve and monitor

Why Save?

- In case of an emergency
- To take advantage of opportunities
- To reach financial goals

The Debit Card

- ATM Card with Bank logo
- Looks just like a credit card, but not a loan, no interest
- Backed only by the checking account behind it
- Widely accepted, can be a good budgeting tool
- Immediate use of money, make sure you don't go overdraft.

When to Use Debit Card vs Credit Card vs Cash

- How you spend money for everyday expenses like groceries, gas, movie theatres and restaurants, clothing should be part of an "overall" spending and savings plan to keep you on track.

Your Credit Score

- Everything you do with your credit accounts affects your credit score including car and school loan
- Creditors extend credit to credit worthy customers
- When you pay your bills on time, you are proving yourself credit worthy
- Banks reward good customers with lower interest rate loans and higher credit lines
- Employers may check your score. A bad score may result in fewer job offers
- Non-installment credit
    - Regular
    - 30-day charge accounts (American Express)
    - Travel and entertainment cards
    - Installment credit
    - Car loan, student loan, home loan
    - Furniture purchase
- Revolving credit
    - Department store cards
- Bank cards: Visa/MasterCard

THREE factors that your Credit Score Says about you

Character – how well you handle financial obligations

Capital – the assets you own, including real estate, savings and investments

Capacity – how much debt you can manage based upon your income

Character

Character is an evaluation of how likely you are to repay your debts. Potential lenders look at your past history, including:

- How well you've handled your money in the past.
- Did you pay bills on time?
- Have you ever filed for bankruptcy?
- How long have you lived at your present address?
- How long have you been at your present job?

Capacity

Capacity looks at how much debt you can handle based on your current financial situation. Lenders want to know whether or not you have been working regularly in a job that will provide enough income to support your credit use.

- Do you have a steady job or income?
- How much do you earn?
- How many other loan payments do you have?
- What are your current living expenses?
- What other debts do you have?
- Do you have children or other dependents that you are supporting?

Advantages of being creditworthy:

- You are more likely to secure favorable rates on loans and credit accounts
- You may qualify for lower auto insurance rates
- You will be able to open utility accounts for your apartment or house without paying large deposits

Challenges of **NOT** being considered creditworthy:

- You will not be able to get loans or credit cards
- You will be charged higher loan and credit card interest rates
- You may be rejected in favor of candidates with better credit histories when you apply to rent an apartment

APPENDIX III
THE POWER OF SAVING

1. Simple interest

Principal x interest rate x time = interest earned

$100,000 x .05 x 1 = $5,000 interest earned every year

2. Compound interest

When your interest compounds, it gets added back to your account and becomes part of your principal. With more principal, the account earns even more interest, which continually compounds into new principal. It's a powerful cycle that really adds up.

In the simple interest example above, $100,000 at a 5% simple APR, earns $5,000 in interest every year.

However, if that interest compounds once a year, the $5,000 interest you earn in year one would be added to the principal at the beginning of year two. By doing this, you earn more interest in year two ($5,250.) and even more in every subsequent year.

$100,000 x .05 x 1 = $5,000 interest earned in year one
$100,050 x .05 x 1 = $5,250 interest earned in year two

The Rule of 72 – Double Down

How fast can your money DOUBLE? The Rule of 72 is a fast way to estimate how long it will take you to double your savings with compound interest. How it is calculated:

72 divided by the interest rate = the number of years needed to double your money. Therefore, if you have a 10% interest rate and want to know how long it will take to double your money, the equation would be:

72 divided by 10 = 7.2 years

APPENDIX IV

Your Three Advisors

1. Lawyer (JD)
   - Estate Planning- protection for Probate, Creditors, execute your wishes
   - Asset Protection – protection from Creditors
   - Litigation – You sue someone or someone sues you
   - Intellectual Property – setup and protect your brand
   - Business Attorney – regular operations of a business, documents and compliance with state and federal laws

American Bar Association Service Center – to find your local state bar
(800) 285-2221
[International (312) 988-5000]
https://www.americanbar.org/about_the_aba/contact/

2. Investment Advisor (CFP, ChFA, etc)
    - Choosing the right investments
    - Education you on what you are investing in and why
    - Planning for Long Term and Short Term
    - May also help with
        - Life Insurance
        - Disability Insurance
        - Long Term Care Insurance

FINRA Investor Complaint Center
http://www.finra.org/
9509 Key West Avenue
Rockville, MD 20850-3329
Phone: (240) 386-HELP (4357)

Problems addressed by FINRA:

- Buy or sell orders
- Brokerage firm or broker
- Insider trading
- Manipulation of security price or volume
- Account transfer
- 401(k), pension or retirement plan
- Investment adviser/financial planner
- Other - Complaints other than those noted in the sections below

3. Certified Public Accountant (CPA)
    - o Taxes, Taxes and more Taxes
    - o Business Structure
    - o Business Plan development
    - o Business management
    - o Personal CFO
    - o Business Consulting and Planning

NASBA – National Associations of the State Board Of Accountants
To find your local state board https://nasba.org/
150 Fourth Ave. North, Ste. 700
Nashville, TN 37219-2417
Phone: (615) 880-4200

APPENDIX V GOAL SETTING

Before the start of the season, before the start of any game, before the start of an athletic career, you set goals. Win the Stanley Cup, Super Bowl, World Series, NBA champs, Gold Medals or NCAA Championships, those are goals! They are concrete and the path to get achieving them is pretty straight forward. Those are team goals. While the Olympics may be individual goals, it still resonates as a goal for the Olympic Team or your Country. Individual goals may be a number of Wins, Hits, Goals, Touchdowns, etc.

Goals for professionals, entrepreneurs, or employees may be slightly less concrete or the path may be indirect. If your goal is to be the CFO of a Publicly Traded company, that is a lofty and achievable goal; however, the path to get there may be direct or may take thousands of little goals.

What about FINANCIAL GOALS?

Basic financial goals revolve around money. Getting it (Earnings), Keeping it (Saving), Using it wisely (Budgets), Growing it (Investments) or Giving it away (Charity.) Any way you want to set your goals there is no right or wrong answer.

How to set your goals is up to you. Whom you chose to help you process your desires, wishes and goals and help you achieve them is up to you.

Once you set your goals, how you get there is the challenge. Start by working backwards. If your goal is to hit .300 in baseball, then start with what is my batting average today. Next, you need to consult with experts on how to improve your batting stance, swing, mental approach to the plate, how you perform against certain teams, pitchers, stadiums, weather etc.

Harvey Mackay recently published an article in his syndicated column that 'Goals require growth to be achieved." He has his own formula for goals.

- Make it Positive - don't set your goal to be "not to strike out so much."
- Be fully Committed.
- Step By Step – By working with your professional team, you can build a program to reach your goals. I recently sat with my investment advisor and said; "this is what I want to have when I retire, here is where I am now, how do I get there?" we then set up a 10-year plan to achieve the goal.
- Appreciate the learning experience – you may have challenges and delays or other hurdles in front of you.

Figure out what does NOT work, what DOES work and why.

- Take them seriously – if you don't, no one else will either.
- Trust your judgment - In addition trust the judgment of your professional advisors/coaches. There is NO rule against asking for help.
- BE AMBITIOUS - there is no sense in achieving a goal that does not require effort, if it seems too big, then break it up into smaller goals along your path.

Mackay's Moral: Don't be afraid to dream big – be afraid not to.

APPENDIX V
STARTING A BUSINESS

1. How to Start a Business
   - Is Entrepreneurship For You?
   - 20 Questions Before Starting
   - 10 Steps to Starting a Business
   - Understand Your Market
     - Business Data & Statistics
       - General Business Statistics
       - Consumer Statistics
       - Demographics
       - Economic Indicators
       - Employment Statistics
       - Income Statistics
       - Money & Interest Rates
       - Production & Sales Statistics
       - Trade Statistics
       - Statistics for Specific Industries

2. Business Types
    - Green Businesses
    - Startups & High Growth Businesses
    - Home-Based Businesses
    - Online Businesses
    - Franchise Businesses
    - Buying Existing Businesses
    - Self Employed & Independent Contractors
    - Women-Owned Businesses
    - Veteran-Owned Businesses
    - People with Disabilities
    - Young Entrepreneurs
    - Encore Entrepreneurs
    - Minority-Owned Businesses
    - Native Americans

3. Find a Mentor or Counselor
4. Write Your Business Plan
    - Executive Summary
    - Company Description
    - Market Analysis
    - Organization & Management
    - Service or Product Line
    - Marketing & Sales
    - Funding Request
    - Financial Projections
    - Appendix
    - How to Make Your Business Plan Stand Out

5. Choose Your Business Structure
    - Sole Proprietorship
    - Limited Liability Company
    - Cooperative
    - Corporation
    - Partnership
    - S Corporation
6. Choose & Register Your Business
    - Choose Your Business Name
    - Register Your Business Name
    - Register With State Agencies
7. Choose Your Business Location & Equipment
    - Tips for Choosing Your Business Location
    - Basic Zoning Laws
    - Home-Based Business Zoning Laws
    - Leasing Commercial Space
    - Buying Government Surplus
    - Leasing Business Equipment
8. Business Licenses & Permits
    - Federal Licenses & Permits
    - State Licenses & Permits
9. Learn About Business Laws
    - Advertising & Marketing Law
    - Employment & Labor Law
    - Finance Law
    - Intellectual Property Law
    - Online Business Law
        - Collecting Sales Tax Online

        - International Online Sales
    - Privacy Law
    - Environmental Regulations
    - Regulation of Financial Contracts
    - Workplace Safety & Health Law
    - Foreign Workers & Employee Eligibility
    - Contact a Government Agency
        - Assistance with Regulatory Compliance
        - Economic Development Agencies

10. Business Financials
    - Estimating Startup Costs
    - Using Personal Finances
    - Preparing Financial Statements
    - Developing a Cash Flow Analysis
    - Breakeven Analysis
    - Borrowing Money for Your Business
    - Is Your Business Fiscally Fit?
11. Finance Your Business
    - Loans
        - SBA Loans
        - Business Loan Application Checklist
        - SBA Loan Application Checklist
        - Acquiring Financing
    - Grants
    - Venture Capital
        - Venture Capital
        - SBIC Directory
    - Business USA Financing Tool

12. Filing & Paying Taxes
    - o Is It A Business or a Hobby?
    - o Obtain Your Federal Business Tax ID
    - o Determine Your Federal Tax Obligations
    - o Determine Your State Tax Obligations
    - o Determine When the Tax Year Starts
13. Hire & Retain Employees

APPENDIX VI MENTORSHIP

Excerpts from thebalancesmb.com "the value of a business-mentor" (Allen/2018) and virgin.com's "10 tips to becoming perfect business mentor"

Learn Why Every Entrepreneur Should Have a Business Mentor

Your friends and family, the online gurus, publications, and even casual acquaintances can provide you with a steady flow of information regarding news, industry developments, and opportunities. Industry analysts, consultants, employees, and good networking contacts can share their expert knowledge with you regarding particular situations and needs you may encounter. However, only a business mentor can truly share wisdom with you on an ongoing basis, and in a manner that can have a direct positive impact on the growth of your business over time.

The generic business advice you'll get from online publications will only go so far, and a good business mentor picks up right where that leaves off.

A business mentor is someone with more entrepreneurial business experience than you, who serves as a trusted confidante over an extended period of time, usually free of charge.

Does this sound a little too good to be true? Well, first and foremost, being a business mentor to an up-and-coming entrepreneur is a great way of giving back to their community, and to society at large when their advice and guidance can have a measurable impact helping their mentees.

Many business mentors may advise people in order to develop their skills as a teacher, manager, strategist, or consultant. Moreover, a true mentorship relationship also works in both directions—your mentor gets to learn about new ideas, strategies and tactics from you, just as you'll learn timeless wisdom from them.

Here are five key benefits of finding a business mentor:

1. Where else are you going to turn?

Once you launch into your own business, there's no boss to turn to for advice or direction when you're in a pinch—maybe not even any employees yet. Although you're flying solo, you don't have to be. Everybody needs a good reliable sounding board, second opinion, and sometimes just emotional support when the times get tough (which they will).

2. They've "been there and done that."

Perhaps the most obvious benefit of finding a business mentor is that you can learn from their previous mistakes and successes. Your mentor doesn't need to have experience in your particular industry—though it helps if they do—so that you're maximizing your opportunities to leverage key relationships. They don't have to be up on the latest trends or technology—you've got other sources for that. Your mentor's role is to share with you lessons from their experience in the hopes that you can learn them quickly and easily.

3. It's (usually) free.

If you're on a tight budget, that's a major factor. While good coaches and consultants may be able to offer some things that a mentor doesn't, it almost always comes at a price, usually of several hundred dollars (or more) each month. Mentors, though, are readily available, free of charge through a number of organizations, such as SCORE (Service Corps Of Retired Executives) and many other groups. Plan on at least treating your mentor to lunch or coffee when you meet together.

4. Expand your social network.

Your mentor, being an experienced businessperson, is likely to have an extensive network, and can offer you access to far more senior decision-makers than you currently have. They will be far more willing to open that network up to you than some casual acquaintance from a networking meeting.

5. A trusted, long-term relationship.

Your mentor has no ulterior motive—no service or product to sell you. That, combined with their experience, creates a good foundation for trust. And as the relationship develops over time, that trust can grow even stronger. Also, your time with them becomes more and more efficient as they become more and more familiar with you and your business.

As you can see, the rewards are potentially great to bring on a business mentor, and the risk is non-existent. You have nothing to lose and everything to gain by finding a good mentor. Every entrepreneur should have one.

There's a decline in the number of businesses starting up in the United States as we see the economy improving. This means less people are starting businesses out of necessity, and instead people are doing so out of passion and because they see an opportunity in the market.

Programs like The Presidential Ambassadors for Global Entrepreneurship are focused on developing the next generation of entrepreneurs, but what can we individually do to help? You may know someone who is interested in starting their own business or embodies the entrepreneurial spirit – perhaps an intern or employee at your company, your neighbor, maybe even your child. Here are some suggestions on how to work with the next generation to set them up for success as a business owner.

While starting a business out of passion rather than necessity sets one up for success initially, the fact remains that many entrepreneurs lack the basic business or leadership skills that are necessary to maintain or grow a business. We see new businesses fail all the time, and the majority of the time it's due to incompetence.

1. Communication – Being able to communicate effectively will help build relationships, problem solve, and convey what a business is and why consumers need whatever is being sold. Unfortunately, many young people are lacking at face-to-face interactions because of social media and text messages. Successful businesses require that people actually speak to one another.

Start with the importance of a professional appearance and introductions (eye contact, handshake) and the importance of the elevator speech. As an entrepreneur, they'll likely have to pitch their business and it's got to be on point in order to compete.

2. Leadership – Look for opportunities to put them in charge. The bottom line is that an entrepreneur is their own boss, and might

eventually be the manager of other people. They need to have experience taking ownership of things and making decisions.

3. Goal setting – Have a conversation to understand what the individual aspires to be. Jot down several goals and have them pick the one that makes the most sense to be their main focus. Figure out what steps are necessary to accomplish this goal and encourage them to start taking action on those steps immediately. Remember, goals can be altered and now's the perfect time to lay some groundwork for a future business.

4. Recognize opportunities – Teaching future entrepreneurs to seek out opportunities and take action on them will directly contribute to their level of future success. Encourage young people to point out small problems or setbacks in their lives or at work. Brainstorm solutions on how to resolve their troubles. This will teach them to focus on creating positive solutions, instead of focusing on the problem itself.

5. Failure – we're often taught that failure is unacceptable. When it comes to entrepreneurship, failure can be a positive thing if there is a lesson learned. Budding entrepreneurs need to understand that at some point, something is not going to go their way – it's part of owning a business.

It's important to be resilient and learn from the situation so they grow as an individual and make better business decisions in the future.

6. Giving back – Every entrepreneur hopes to be successful one day. Understanding the importance of giving back will help the next generation stay humble during periods of success and it will teach them that a successful business provides benefits to more than just

its owner.

7. Independence – Having the freedom to make your own decisions is often considered to be one of the greatest benefits of entrepreneurship. The key to independence is confidence. In many cases, confidence must be learned. In the case of a future entrepreneur, they're going to learn to believe in their own abilities from acting on challenges, seeing the results and being praised and respected by others.

8. Financial literacy – This is one area where entrepreneurs really struggle. It's one thing to manage your own bank account, but what about managing the money coming in and out of a business? At work, let an aspiring entrepreneur co-own the department's budget. It's also a good idea to prep them for the fact that they will likely need help in this area; an accountant can serve as an advisor on where a business's money is going vs. where it should be going.

BIBLIOGRAPHY

- Motley Fool.com; 6 Financial Mistakes That Are Ruining Your Credit ; Kailey Fralick Jul 23; https://www.fool.com/credit-cards/2018/07/23/6-financial-mistakes-that-are-ruining-your-credit.aspx

- Motley Fool.com; 3 Smart Ways to Save Money on Your Next Car; Matthew Frankel, CFP ; Sep 13, 2018; https://www.fool.com/retirement/2018/09/13/3-smart-ways-to-save-money-on-your-next-car.aspx

- Investopedia.com; what is a Budget? Budgeting Terms and Tips; Reviewed by Julia Kagen ; Updated Jan 17, 2018; https://www.investopedia.com/terms/b/budget.asp

- Investopedia.com; How to Find a Financial Advisor/Planner ; https://www.investopedia.com/updates/find-financial-advisor-planner.

- Investopedia.com; https://www.investopedia.com/financial-edge/0312/why-athletes-go-broke.aspx; Why Athletes Go Broke ; Tim Parker ; Mar 5, 2012

- Nerdwallet ; Associated Press Former stars explain why NFL players go broke, and what you can learn;; Oct. 10, 2017 https://www.businessinsider.com/ap-liz-weston-why-nfl-players-go-broke-and-what-you-can-learn-2017-10

- Investopedia.com; What do Financial Advisors Do; https://www.investopedia.com/articles/personal-finance/050815/what-do-financial-advisers-do.asp

- https://www.pressreader.com/usa/the-arizona-republic/20181224/281621011449525 Dec 24, 2018 - Goals require growth to be achieved

- Investopedia.com Risk Tolerance ; https://www.investopedia.com/articles/pf/07/risk_tolerance.asp

- Motley Fool.com; Budgeting 101: How to Start Budgeting for the First Time; Christy Bieber ; Apr 21, 2018 at 10:16AM; https://www.fool.com/investing/2018/04/21/budgeting-101-how-to-start-budgeting-for-the-first.aspx?source=isesitlnk0000001&mrr=1.00

- Pacific Standard Magazine; How We Set Up Our Professional Athletes to Fail; Author: Sam Riches; Publish date:Feb 18, 2014 https://psmag.com/economics/professional-athletes-set-fail-74247

- Forbes.com; Curt Schilling And Why Athletes Make Such Poor Financial Decisions; Monte Burke ; SportsMoney; May 25, 2012, 12:50pm; https://www.forbes.com/sites/monteburke/2012/05/25/curt-schilling-and-why-athletes-make-such-poor-financial-decisions/#12ddfb9531b4

- American Psychological Association; Exercise and Sport Psychology Newsletter; May 2016; https://www.apa.org/about/division/div47.aspx

- Floyd Little, Interview for "Beyond the Game", (Silverlight Films, 2017)

- Securities and Exchange Commission; SEC.gov https://www.investor.gov/research-before-you-invest/research/five-questions-ask-before-you-invest

- By Kareem Abdul-Jabbar; 20 Things I Wish I'd Known When I Was 30; When I was thirty, Apr 30, 2013; https://www.esquire.com/news-politics/news/a22394/kareem-things-i-wish-i-knew/

- Paychex Inc; https://www.paychex.com/articles/startup/employee-to-entrepreneur-businesses-start;

- Pro Athletes Prove Why You Should Stick To A Financial Playbook; Aug 16, 2017, Zach Conway https://www.forbes.com/sites/zachconway/2017/08/16/pro-athletes-prove-why-you-should-stick-to-a-financial-playbook/

- NCAA, http://www.ncaa.org/about/resources/research/estimated-probability-competing-college-athletics; 2018

- https://www.thebalancesmb.com/the-value-of-a-business-mentor-1200818 (Allen/2018)

- NCAA; http://www.ncaa.org/about/resources/research/estimated-probability-competing-professional-athletics; 2018

- Michelle Gill; Value of and contributions of the participation in intercollegiate athletics on the personal development of community college-aged students; (2015) http://digitalcommons.unl.edu/cehsedaddiss/232

- Danny Schayes; Fast Broke: Learn the reason athletes go broke; Nomad CEO Publishing; isbn 13:978-1502869715;

- https://www.virgin.com/entrepreneur/10-tips-becoming-perfect-business-mentor

- https://www.sba.gov/business-guide/

- Money 101; Visa Practical Money Skills; https://www.practicalmoneyskills.com ; (2018)

- Robert Pagliarini ; Why athletes go broke: The myth of the dumb jock; MoneyWatch; https://www.cbsnews.com/news/why-athletes-go-broke-the-myth-of-the-dumb-jock; (2013)

- Jonathan Miller CPA; https://www.forbes.com; want-to-retire-early-take-a-cue-from-the-pro-baller-playbook. (2016)

- Jonathan Miller, CPA; https://www.cnbc.con; for-athletes-like-sergio-garcia-tax-season-brings-extra-burdens (2017)
- Jonathan Miller, CPA; NFL Rookie year; Life after football; Interview WBEZ; (2015) http://www.sportsfinancial.org/nfl-rookie-yearlife-after-football-wbezs-morning-shift/
- Jonathan Miller, CPA; Professional Athletes Retirment Conundrum; Chief Investment Officer Magazine; http://www.ai-ciodigital.com/ai-cio; (2016)
- Susan Johnson Taylor; interview with Jonathan Miller , CPA; https://money.usnews.com/money/personal-finance/articles; (2016) 22/what-pro-athletes-can-teach-us-about-retirement-planning
- Amy Armstrong; The Suit Magazine; Don't Blow It; interview with Jonathan Miller, CPA (2016)
- Jonathan Miller,CPA; Wall Street Journal on Advising Professional Athletes ; https://www.wsj.com/articles/SB10001424127887323419604578573341985977374 via @WSJ.
- https://www.cnbc.com/2015/04/23/maybe-floyd-mayweathers-spending-is-the-key-to-winning.htmlMaybe Floyd Mayweather's spending is the key to winning; Robert Frank (2015)
- Sheth, Hela & M. Babiak, Kathy. (2010). Beyond the Game: Perceptions and Practices of Corporate Social Responsibility in the Professional Sport Industry. Journal of

Business Ethics. 91. 433-450. 10.1007/s10551-009-0094-0. (2010)

- Babiak, Kathy & Mills, Brian & Tainsky, Scott & Juravich, Matthew. (2012). An Investigation Into Professional Athlete Philanthropy:
- www.growingagreenerworld.com/jason-brown-football-player-to-farmer/2019
- https://www.sec.gov/litigation/admin/2017/34-79991.pdf

ABOUT THE AUTHOR

Jonathan Miller CPA

President and Shareholder, Jonathan Miller, CPA, PC

Founder and Managing Member, Starcross Management, LLC

Co-Founder, Sports Financial Advisors Association

Founder, The Just 1 Project

Jonathan Miller, a native of Los Angeles, California, currently resides in Paradise Valley, Arizona. He has over 30 years' experience as a Certified Public Accountant in business and tax services.

Through his consulting services, Jonathan is able to integrate his four core capabilities: strategic business planning, corporate structure, tax planning and compliance to provide you or your business with solutions that fit your specific need. Jonathan is also experienced working with CEO's, Professional Athletes and Entertainers as a Business Manager.

Over the past 30 years Jonathan's commitment to education of student and professional athletes has grown to include a 501c(3) Non Profit, the Just One Project; a 501c(6) organization, The Sports Financial Advisors Association; the founding of StarCross Management, LLC, a sports and entertainment management company; and associate production of a full length documentary

"Beyond The Game." Jonathan is also a Certified Financial Education Instructor with the National Financial Educators Council. His goal is to ensure that athlete financial disasters are mitigated and eliminated.

Find out more at www.millerjcpa.com; www.starcrossllc.com; www.beyondthegamefilm.com; www.thejust1project.org.

www.ingramcontent.com/pod-product-compliance
Lightning Source LLC
Chambersburg PA
CBHW031942190326
41519CB00007B/619

* 9 7 8 1 9 4 5 8 4 9 7 6 3 *